D1022247

ALSO BY CAROLINE MYSS

Books

Anatomy of the Spirit

*Defy Gravity**

Entering the Castle

Invisible Acts of Power

Sacred Contracts

Why People Don't Heal and How They Can

CDs/DVDs

Channeling Grace

*Defy Gravity**

Finding Your Sacred Contract

The Language of Archetypes

*What Makes Us Healthy?**

*Available from Hay House

Please visit:

Hay House USA: **www.hayhouse.com**®
Hay House Australia: **www.hayhouse.com.au**
Hay House UK: **www.hayhouse.co.uk**
Hay House South Africa: **www.hayhouse.co.za**
Hay House India: **www.hayhouse.co.in**

Archetypes

Who Are You?

Caroline Myss

HAY HOUSE, INC.
Carlsbad, California • New York City
London • Sydney • Johannesburg
Vancouver • Hong Kong • New Delhi

Copyright © 2013 by Archetypes Publishing LLC

Published and distributed in the United States by: Hay House, Inc.: www.hayhouse. com® • *Published and distributed in Australia by:* Hay House Australia Pty. Ltd.: www.hayhouse.com.au • *Published and distributed in the United Kingdom by:* Hay House UK, Ltd.: www.hayhouse.co.uk • *Published and distributed in the Republic of South Africa by:* Hay House SA (Pty), Ltd.: www.hayhouse.co.za • *Distributed in Canada by:* Raincoast: www.raincoast.com • *Published in India by:* Hay House Publishers India: www.hayhouse.co.in

Interior design: Celia Fuller-Vels

All rights reserved. No part of this book may be reproduced by any mechanical, photographic, or electronic process, or in the form of a phonographic recording; nor may it be stored in a retrieval system, transmitted, or otherwise be copied for public or private use—other than for "fair use" as brief quotations embodied in articles and reviews—without prior written permission of the publisher.

The author of this book does not dispense medical advice or prescribe the use of any technique as a form of treatment for physical, emotional, or medical problems without the advice of a physician, either directly or indirectly. The intent of the author is only to offer information of a general nature to help you in your quest for emotional and spiritual well-being. In the event you use any of the information in this book for yourself, which is your constitutional right, the author and the publisher assume no responsibility for your actions.

Library of Congress Cataloging-in-Publication Data

Myss, Caroline M.
 Archetypes : who are you? / Caroline Myss.
  p. cm.
 ISBN 978-1-4019-4108-6 (hardcover : alk. paper) -- ISBN 978-1-4019-4110-9 (ebk)
 1. Archetype (Psychology) 2. Self-actualization (Psychology) I. Title.
 BF175.5.A72M97 2013
 155.2'64--dc23
                                2012038560

Hardcover ISBN: 978-1-4019-4108-6
Digital ISBN: 978-1-4019-4110-9

16 15 14 13   4 3 2 1
1st edition, January 2013

Printed in the United States of America

Contents

To Cristina Carlino,
a sister and friend
With love and gratitude

Foreword

Archetypes have fascinated me since I first read *Women Who Run with the Wolves* by Clarissa Pinkola Estés 20 years ago. I was further educated in archetypes by Bill Moyers, who covered them in some of his PBS specials. But it was *Sacred Contracts* by Caroline Myss that creatively blew open the idea of archetypes and how they affect every aspect of our life. In the decade since the book came out, I have discussed archetypes with anyone who would listen, including Caroline, who has become a dear friend and soul sister. We met at an event at which she was speaking. At the time, I was the CEO of philosophy, a skin-care company I had founded, and when the organizers of the event asked me to sponsor it, I immediately agreed—provided I could meet with Caroline privately, to talk about my very sick friend Dana Reeve. (Among her many talents, Caroline is a gifted medical intuitive.) I am so blessed that the meeting worked out, as Caroline and I have had a loving bond ever since.

Fast-forward to 2009, when I received a phone call from the company that had taken over philosophy, informing me that my creative services were no longer needed but I could stay on with the honorary title of executive chairman as long as I stayed out of the new CEO's way. Heartbroken and humiliated, I resigned and spent the next month facedown on my bed crying. Despite all my professional success, I felt like a failure. That one phone call had stolen my identity. But as it turned out, that phone call was the best thing that could have happened.

About a month later, I did what any normal woman does when she has time on her hands: I started cleaning out my closet.

I sat on the floor and began sorting through the costume party of clothes I had accumulated over the years. The piles I loved were items that were Artistic—feminine, floaty, creative, and ethereal. Then there was the pile of Visionary uniforms—multiples of the same shoes, pants, and T-shirts that I bought 10 or 20 of at a time. On the other side of the coin was the pile of high-priced, tailor-made, often bejeweled suits of armor for the boardroom fit for a Queen; I owned many of these, but hated them all and remembered vividly the discomfort I felt every time I had worn them. Same for the pile of Caregiver mommy stretch elastic. Those outfits never were me, and yet they dominated that closet floor.

There I sat, looking at the story of my life as seen through the lens of my closet, when light broke through the darkness of my despair and my third company, Archetypes, Inc., was born.

It was as if the Visionary who conceived philosophy was awakened from a deep sleep. What I saw were piles of different archetypes. Some of the piles fit my true archetypes, and most didn't. I began to think about how I had been derailed in the previous decade by trying to adapt to an archetype (a Caregiver) that wasn't authentic to me. I thought about how I had been role-playing as a Queen/Executive without ever being fully comfortable in that role, and especially in the clothes that came with it.

The truth that became apparent from that exercise that day on the floor of my closet was that the empty feeling I had—despite having achieved great personal and professional success—was born out of not living my archetypes.

Looking back, I see that I was not suffering from a case of stolen identity but rather going through an archetype crisis. The Queen/Executive was dead but the Creative Visionary who had founded philosophy was not. What's more, my next venture had been under my nose all the time. I wanted to create a social platform where people could learn all about the fascinating subject of archetypes and how they can transform our lives and our relationships. ArchetypeMe would help people make empowered choices through the prism of their individual archetypes.

The new company gave me a chance to join forces with Caroline Myss. For over 25 years, Caroline has been teaching students about the power of archetypes. Now, with this book, she is going to teach you. You are going to discover how archetypes begin shaping our lives from the moment we are born. You will learn why some people, clothes, and relationships fit like a glove and others bring you deep discomfort. You will, for the first time, be able to look at your closet, your home, your career, and your significant relationships and ask yourself one simple question: *Am I living my archetype?* In other words, am I living the life I was destined to live, the life of my true self?

The most beautiful discovery about archetypes is that they awaken you to synchronicity, to the signs, symbols, and meaningful coincidences that come into our lives and get our immediate attention. They say stop, go, or stay still, but whatever the directive you know intuitively that you need to listen. Heeding the blessings and warnings called out by these signs is deeply empowering. And with that, miracles are born in your life one by one by one.

Discovering archetypes was one of those miracles for me. Meeting Caroline was another. I hope they will be for you, too.

With grace and gratitude,
Cristina Carlino
New York, 2012

Introduction

I have long believed that it is impossible for us to know who we truly are unless we understand archetypes and, more specifically, our own personal archetypes, because archetypes are the psychic lenses through which we view ourselves and the world around us. As a society we have been on a quest to understand how we function psychologically, what makes us the way we are, and what makes us heal. These questions have awakened a need in us to not only be aware that archetypes influence us but how they express themselves in our individual lives. Archetypes are the new language of power.

I was well into the writing of a different book when Cristina Carlino asked me to drop what I was doing and write this book, as well as contribute to the website she was developing. Cristina described her vision of networks of people—*Arch-e-mates,* she called them—linking up with one another through their archetypal patterns. She saw endless possibilities in how people could improve their health, their relationships, their overall well-being—their whole world—if they could grasp the true essence of who they were. I didn't hesitate to agree to Cristina's proposal, as I knew that making this material available to a wider audience would be transformational. Together, *Archetypes: Who Are You?* and the website **www.ArchetypeMe.com** offer an interactive vessel for stepping into the power of your archetypes and using their magnetism to assist you in opening to the full expression of your life.

The time has come for our society to make a quantum leap in awareness and acknowledge the central role of intuition. Archetypes are the vocabulary of intuition, and the more familiar we are with them, the more clearly we will resonate with our own intuition. Archetypes speak to us in a language of myths and symbols, perfectly suited to a society that has become fluent in high-tech code, instant messages, and Twitter-speak. The only difference is that archetypes originate in our cosmic intelligence and not in our technical awareness. But it was inevitable that one day our rational intellect would find a way to engage with our intuitive intelligence, and through the medium of archetypes, it has.

Archetypes are the keys to our personal power. I have witnessed dramatic changes when people awaken to this power. More than once, I have seen them come to the realization that their need for time alone was not because they are antisocial but because they have the Hermit archetype, which compels them to seek silence and solitude in order to sustain their spirit. I have watched other people discover that they have a passion to be in nature not because they want to get out of the city but because they identify with the Nature Child, an archetypal expression of the soul of the natural world. Upon discovering which archetypes are guiding your life, you step into the core of your being, perhaps for the first time. It's as if you have finally put on the clothing you were destined to wear.

Though I firmly believe that the language of archetypes is becoming our next new language, there was a time not so long ago when I wasn't so sure. The day I gave my first lecture on the subject, I worried that I might not be able to communicate clearly that archetypes are universal patterns of power emerging from our myths and beliefs, and that these myths and beliefs, in turn, invisibly weave their influential threads into the way we view every aspect of our lives. I was doubly hesitant about speaking because I knew that the field of archetypes came with its own vocabulary, one associated with the inner realm of the psyche. For our rational, logical, scientific society, information that is introduced as "powerful but invisible" generally doesn't stand a chance of gaining much credibility.

But much to my surprise, I discovered that a few simple examples of easily recognized archetypes immediately created the bridge I needed between the literal world in which we live and the mythic or symbolic world that is the power zone of the archetypes. I asked the women in the audience, "How many of you always knew you were going to be mothers?" A majority of them raised their hands. I then asked, "How did you know that?" Most just shrugged their shoulders as if to say, "I just knew it because that's who I am, and that's what I was meant to do—be a Mother."

Then I asked the audience, "How many of you are natural-born Adventurers?" Several men raised their hands, along with a few women. "And how many of you would consider yourselves Warriors?" I asked. Even more men raised their hands. I was amazed, as I had thought that the victorious Warrior story was more a woman's fantasy than a man's. But that day I realized that many men find it sexy to imagine themselves as modern-day warriors like the Navy SEALs.

By the time I discussed the Healer and Hermit archetypes, audience members were no longer asking questions about archetypes in general but rather "What are my archetypes?" and "How do I identify my archetypal patterns?" The atmosphere in the room was electric, sparking with a level of curiosity I had never before experienced in an audience. They would have stayed all night in that lecture hall if I had let them.

Later, over dinner with friends, I could not stop talking about the explosion of enthusiasm in that room. No other subject I had ever taught had elicited such a response. What was it about archetypes that triggered that reaction? As I thought about it more, the answer seemed obvious: Archetypal patterns hold the key to the real you. They somehow know more about you than you know about yourself. By identifying and exploring your own archetypal patterns, you come to understand your true self.

Archetypes have always been the engine of the human unconscious, but you could live your whole life and not know that. Archetypal patterns are like a door into a hidden realm, a parallel reality. Discovering this parallel reality in which archetypes reside and learning about your particular archetypes is a way of meeting yourself, perhaps for the first time.

My hope is that you will find this inner journey as life changing as I have.

Caroline Myss
Oak Park, 2012

CHAPTER 1

Archetypes: The New Inner-net

If I said to you, "See that man over there? He's my Hero," or "That woman is the Perfect Mom," I know without a doubt that you would understand exactly what I was communicating to you about two people you had never met. With just three words—*Hero* and *Perfect Mom*—I would have awakened in you two complete archives of myths and symbols that you automatically associate with those terms. In seconds, these two people would cease to be strangers, as your psyche wrapped them in stories, fairy tales, and your own memories. The man would instantly take on the appearance of a super-strong Hero able to face any adversary. Despite knowing nothing else about him, you would instantly trust him. After all, Heroes don't betray the women they're sent to rescue—at least not in the fairy tales we know and love, right?

The Hero would be a Lone Ranger type: solitary, intense, a one-woman man who would sweep you off your feet. (How could he be a real Hero if he were messing around with other women?) Every woman wants a Hero of her own. From ancient Greek warriors like Hercules, Odysseus, and Achilles to legendary figures like Robin Hood and Braveheart to real-life Heroes like the Navy SEALs who risked their lives to take down Osama bin Laden, they enthrall us with their exploits. And now we've added Heroines to the paragons of heroism we admire, with contemporary eco-warriors like Karen Silkwood and Erin Brockovich. Their strength is moral courage.

Heroes and Heroines are the most popular movie figures of our day. Make a movie about Batman, Spider-Man, Superman, or Wonder Woman, and it will be the #1 draw on opening week. Why? It's simple: We not only love our Heroes and Heroines, we *need* them. A society without Heroes is a defeated society. They are our power icons, symbolizing to the world that we are invincible as a nation.

You, too, have at least one Hero. If not, you long for one. You may not be in the market for your own personal comic-book figure come to life, but the idea of having someone to rely on who gallops in to save the day—psychologically, if not literally—is right up there on most people's list of necessities for a happy and secure life. We all share this need for Heroes in some way because it is built into our emotional DNA. What we call *human nature* is also our *archetypal nature*. Certain qualities and characteristics are inherently human: caring for others, protection of the young, loyalty, the ability to love, the need to safeguard home and family. And all these innately human qualities are represented by archetypes, by these universal, impersonal patterns of influence that reside in the collective unconscious—in the psyche of the species, as it were, that we share with every other human being.

Consider the archetype of the *Perfect Mom*. You don't need to meet the woman I'm speaking about to flesh out an idea of her in your imagination. The words *Perfect Mom* pack a powerful punch, especially in our society, where we have commercially enhanced this archetype beyond its already deeply rooted sentimental meaning. The instant someone tells you that a woman is a Perfect Mom, you immediately picture a great cook with a charming, well-ordered home, who helps her kids with their homework, attends all their sporting events, listens to their problems, hosts sleepovers with their friends— and bakes brownies. Even if the words *Perfect Mom* bring up painful associations with a not-so-perfect upbringing, you still have the projection of the ideal Mother figure firmly planted in your psyche.

So how do those words—*Hero* and *Perfect Mom*—communicate so much visual, emotional, intellectual, and mythic information to us? They carry the power they do because they are archetypes, psychic power patterns in the unconscious mind. Although archetypes are collective symbols that everyone in the culture shares, they can also speak to us individually, as personal archetypal patterns that are the foundation of our beliefs, drives, motivations, and actions, organizing and energizing all our relationships in life. Archetypes are the power images we identify with as children. The Athlete or the Artist or the Actor or the Princess or even, sad to say, the Victim or the Vampire represents a complex of stories and myths that we somehow imagine happening in our own life. We are drawn to movies, books, and video games with characters that represent our power images. Little girls dress up as Princesses and Wonder Woman, little boys as Batman and Warriors. Archetypal identification begins early.

As we grow up, we continue to pattern our lives around these images, unconsciously living our archetypes. I think of archetypes as our energy companions. From birth, we are living out the archetypal patterns that are active in our psyche. As human beings we love patterns—they bring order to our lives. We are continually scanning our world for patterns, particularly in people, because we know intuitively that if we understand someone's behavior patterns we understand how she relates to herself, to her life, and to us. We understand a person better, for instance, if we know that she is essentially an Intellectual; that explains, for example, why she loves foreign films and biographies of great historic figures. We appreciate our friends for understanding that because we have the Athlete archetype, working out each day is vital to our physical, mental, and emotional well-being. Exercising is more than a hobby; it's part of who we are at our core.

You may not be conscious of it, but you have been doing "archetypal power readings" of people since you were a child—only you probably think of it as labeling someone or even judging them, if the label is a negative one. People watching is all about archetypal power readings—scanning strangers and instantly gathering information about their lives. What you are scanning for are what I call archetypal "fun facts"—common traits that are dead giveaways as to what a person is like. The Bad Boy has tattoos that reflect a tough image. A Vampire has that look about her that says she's in need of someone's energy to drain. The Diva, of course, is nearly unmistakable. And Eye Candy is obvious, but the Good Samaritan can be a bit tricky to spot. You never know what type of package the Good Samaritan may come in, which is, in itself, a characteristic of this archetype. We are continually downloading these intuitive energy snapshots of people into our archetypal scrapbooks.

We can't help reading the archetypes of one another: it's a natural part of our intuitive survival mechanism. We trust patterns that are familiar to us—archetypes we intuitively recognize. When we don't trust someone, it's because we can't get a fix on her archetype or we've encountered someone else with that archetype before and we don't like how that archetype behaves.

We are wired to "speak archetypes" just as surely as we are wired to crawl, walk, and communicate. Archetypes, symbols, and myths comprise aspects of our intuitive intelligence. We are naturally intuitive, as we require these senses for our very survival. The fight-or-flight response and the highly reactive "gut instinct" are examples of organic intuitive intelligence that we rely on all the time. Similarly, you sense or read archetypes intuitively, even though you may be unaware that you have an inherent skill at understanding or responding to the language of myths and symbols. But recall that the language of your imagination consists of myths and symbols, and fantasizing is one of the earliest languages in the child's mind. We are in touch with our imagination and dreams before we engage with logic and reason.

You were in mythic contact with your world before you learned to read and write about it. You had invisible friends, and you imagined visiting schools where wizards learned their craft. And it was real for you, at least for a time. Even though as an adult you realize those mythic places don't exist in the physical sense, you still cling to them in your psyche. They represent your sacred psychic space, your personal archetypal territory.

The language of archetypes is the universal language of the human soul, psychically uniting us all through what the Swiss psychiatrist Carl Jung called the collective unconscious. Jung saw archetypes as the quintessential navigational tool of the psyche, providing a gateway between the conscious mind and the unconscious that could help us in becoming integrated human beings.

He also noticed that archetypes frequently partner with other archetypes, which accounts for the variety of ways in which an archetype may express itself, depending on the individual. One woman I know, for example, has a very strong Artist archetype. She has been in touch with her artistic talent from childhood and stepped into her "artistic skin" naturally, easily, and gracefully. Everything she does, from how she dresses to how she sets her dinner table, has an artistic touch. She truly exists in harmony with her Artist archetype, without giving it conscious thought.

But in another person I know, the Artist archetype is blended with other archetypal patterns to form a very different type of power unit. His childhood was not quite as abundant as our first Artist's; thus, his Artist took on the qualities of the Starving Artist, an aspect of the Artist archetype made famous by painters like Toulouse-Lautrec and van Gogh. This man's inability to fully believe in his talent continually diminished his self-esteem, leading him to withdraw into a Fragile Child archetype. The Fragile Child partnered with his Starving Artist to produce a constant narrative of fear within him. Like a mental sound system he could not turn off, it played all day, telling him he could not survive in the world as the kind of Creative Artist he once envisioned himself as being. He eventually returned home to take a part-time job as a house painter and handyman. In order to pay the bills, he had to revise his inner myth, the story he told himself about who he "really" was and what was happening to him. He now told himself that he was just painting houses until he could save enough money to take the art classes he needed. So long as the Starving Artist and the Fragile Child archetypes were in charge of his inner myths, he would never leave home, so powerful are the myths contained in our archetypes. He would always have the option, however, of revitalizing his inner Creative Artist. The only thing standing in his way was his fear that he lacked the talent required to make it in the competitive world of art. Archetypes will always find expression in one way or another—in his case, house painting became a rest stop until courage came along.

The Emerging Inner-net

What Jung referred to as the collective unconscious, I think of as our *Inner-net,* a high-speed, interconnected psychic network that links us to every other human being through a vast system of archetypes. Each archetype is its own computer program, complete with its own particular set of myths and its own reservoir of symbols and cultural legends associated with each of those myths.

Now picture Earth and imagine that there are billions of lines crisscrossing the surface, serving as a rapid-fire network transferring all human psychic activity at an infinitely fast rate. Every thought, feeling, sensation, and human vibration is transmitted instantaneously across this archetypal grid, transferring the one common ingredient of the human experience: power. Whatever you do, say, think, calculate, consider, or wear is carried out with power in mind. Power is the single ingredient common to your every human action, from the moment of your birth to your death. Everything about your life is a power negotiation, with all of that power transitioning through this archetypal grid.

Think about why you make the choices you make, and what motivates you to act as you do. At the end of the day, your choices are based upon power calculations: Will what I say or do in this moment empower me or disempower me? Should I keep quiet? Speak up? Be honest? Should I act on my intuition or seek out more information? What's my best course of action here? Something as simple as getting a second opinion on a restaurant your friend has suggested can be intimidating. *Better to just agree and go along with the group,* most people think.

But why do we reduce every choice to a power calculation that gets transmitted across the energetic power grid? Because we're all connected, all part of the same web of life. We are born already connected to this Inner-net, this energetic power grid, arriving with a backpack filled with truths and wisdom inherent to the human experience. This is what we innately know, such as a deep understanding of right and wrong. It's in our cellular DNA. We aren't aware of these DNA truths from birth, however; we gradually become aware of them as we mature. This is sacred knowledge, which needs to be awakened, stirred from within, and recognized intuitively, not with the rational mind. If you have ever wondered what the real purpose of your life is, or said to yourself, "I need to find out what's really important to me," then you have already begun the process. Those inner stirrings are an invitation to awaken, to go in search of the more authentic you.

We are drawn to stories about ancient Heroes who go off on the archetypal Hero's Journey, the solo quest to uncover your true self. In finding a route to that precious sacred knowledge of who you really are, you reach a place of empowerment. This is the essence of genuine self-esteem, the holy grail of the inner quest.

Consider for a second the question around which I wrote this book: *Who are you, really?* We all ask ourselves *Who am I?* many times in many ways throughout our life, but we need the right language to excavate the answers from deep within us. We ask that question because we are actually seeking to understand the reason why we were given the gift of this life: *For what reason was I born?* This question marks an archetypal passageway, a turning point in our desire to know ourselves more deeply. It symbolizes a maturing in which we shift from defining ourselves by what we *own* to wanting to know ourselves by what we can *do* or *be* or *contribute*. Do I have the Artist in me? Was I born to be a Visionary? To know the deeper truth about yourself requires traveling to your interior on the power of your archetypes.

Connecting to Your Archetypes and the Inner-net

In this book, I introduce you to the Inner-net and to ten archetypal patterns that reflect the power trends of our times: the Advocate, the Artist/Creative, the Athlete, the Caregiver, the Fashionista, the Intellectual, the Queen/Executive, the Rebel, the Spiritual Seeker, and the Visionary. Each archetype is presented as the representative of an archetypal family, a team of archetypes with similar patterns. These general archetypal families cover both men and women. The Caregiver, for example, is the lead member of the Caring family, a team associated with nurturing that includes the Mother, the Rescuer, the Teacher, the Healer, and the Companion. Similarly, the Rebel comes from a family of archetypes that includes the Maverick, the Warrior, and the Hero. All members of an archetype family share a body of characteristics, but there are subtle distinctions between the members that sometimes cause confusion. People frequently have difficulty distinguishing between the Healer and the Rescuer, for example, as both have an inherent need to respond to those seeking aid. However, the initiation of the Healer—known as the Wounded Healer's Journey—is unique to the Healer and not a part of the Rescuer archetype. (Not all archetypes have a journey of initiation. Initiation is a sacred ritual associated with archetypes that serve in a sacred role, such as healing.) The Wounded Healer's Journey is an important initiation that many of you may recognize.

The journey of the Wounded Healer begins with a "wound." The wound could take the form of a serious accident, an illness, or life circumstances that cause the person to lose most of her earthly possessions, leaving her the choice to collapse under the strain or "take up her bed and walk." The Wounded Healer's wound brings the person to a do-or-die choice, offering the person the opportunity to completely transform her relation to power. Up to that point, she defined power as something external—status, money, fame, security, and belief in her own invincibility. The wound destroys the illusion that any of that is truly empowering, showing that emptiness, the false promise of external definitions of power. The choice for the Wounded Healer is to shed all her beliefs about power and earthly security and discover an alternate healing paradigm. She comes to understand that her wound can only be healed in full partnership with her spirit.

This explains why many Wounded Healers experience remarkable recoveries from illnesses or situations that would have sent other people to the grave. In coming through the ordeal healed, the Wounded Healer is empowered to assist others in healing their wounds.

The Ten Archetypes

The ten archetypes in the book embody the primary power issues that define women today, including their underlying struggles with personal empowerment. Ten years ago, the list of defining archetypes would have been different, and it may change again ten years from now. But in the world as we know it today, the modern woman is likely to consider herself a Professional, or if not a Professional then someone looking for her place in the world. The current definition of *Professional* has expanded beyond someone employed in a practice or corporate setting to include anyone who has mastered a craft or created a home-based business. Today's woman is also likely to see herself as a Caregiver, whether or not she is a mother. Her Caregiver may have a rebellious streak, simply by virtue of adapting to life in a world so vastly different from the one in which previous generations of women lived, or she may be a woman in whom the Rebel is a full-time force. Many women today find themselves called to make a difference in the world, as Advocates for their communities or as Eco-Advocates—environmental activists—an archetype that has taken shape only recently in the collective unconscious. (Mother Nature didn't used to need human beings to represent her cause within political circles, but these are the times we now live in.) Women Visionaries play a greater role today as engines of societal change. And more women have become Athletes, as fitness and exercise have become prime values in today's world. As society shifts, so do the archetypal images that govern our Inner-net, altering our definitions of beauty, power, and life goals. Today's Fashionista, for example, introduces us to ways to feel good about ourselves through clothing, makeup, hairstyles, and shoes.

In addition to reflecting contemporary power themes, the ten archetypes in the book embody the more pressing personal challenges facing women today. Personal challenges are archetypal because they, too, originate in our archetypal patterns. No one is born with healthy self-esteem, yet our level of self-esteem directs everything we do in life. Women in particular face the challenge of developing this inner sense of power and personal identity. Without that essential core of self-esteem, you will be unable to hear your intuitive guidance. You won't trust the Intellectual in you as it engages with new ideas. You will tune out the Fashionista archetype when it sprinkles your imagination with ideas about creating a new line of clothing or jewelry. You will dismiss the intuitive instructions or suggestions as if they were a bad dream, with a thought like *I could never do that. What if I fail?* or some other excuse coming from low self-esteem. Few forces in life have the positive authority of genuine self-esteem, or the negative effect of a lack of self-esteem.

Archetypes communicate psychically, through hunches, intuitive hits, gut instincts, "chills" running up and down your spine, and other physical sensations. I know how to read the fluid language of my own intuition, as I am comfortable with these inner sensations. They are not at odds with my five senses but rather their perfect complement. My intellect relies on my intuition in a finely tuned working partnership.

Archetypal patterns filter into every aspect of your life, so it's important to discover how they express themselves in your everyday decisions and routines. Your archetypes influence your spending habits, how you shop, and what you buy or not. They influence the quality of your relationships, and who you are attracted to and why. And they influence recurring issues: arguments you seem to have over and over, difficulties at work that keep cropping up, and other patterns that repeat themselves. Anything that repeats is a clue to what archetypes are operating in your life.

And finally, the ten archetypes profiled in the book reflect the collective mythic challenges of our times. We need Visionaries more than ever, because we need to envision new models of energy, new technologies, and new ways of cooperating with our environment. Spiritual Seekers, too, are changing with the times. For women and men who are drawn to a spiritual life, the world itself is a new type of monastery. Today's spiritual practitioners often view their work as a calling, whatever the field. Together with the Athlete, the Advocate, the Artist/Creative, the Caregiver, the Fashionista, the Intellectual, the Queen/Executive, and the Rebel, they form a balanced representation of today's contemporary archetypal family.

CHAPTER 2

Your Personal Journey

The more you know about how archetypes work, the more easily you can observe their influence on your thoughts, your attitudes, your behavior, and your personal myths and symbols. When you begin to explore your archetypes, questions often arise, not the least of which is *How many archetypes do I have?* In this chapter, I'll address the most frequently asked questions about establishing a relationship with your archetypes.

How many archetypes and symbols exist in the universe?

There are an infinite number of archetypes in the human collective unconscious. Many, like the Mother and the Healer and the Hero, are ancient archetypes that are universal and timeless. Others are new ones that we create as we continue to evolve. Among the new archetypes for the Internet Age are the Networker, the Hacker, and the Geek. They are expressions of our time and therefore may evolve out of consciousness as rapidly as they popped in, but still they illustrate the point that the realm of archetypes is interactive. So long as we continue evolving, so also will the character and complexity of the archetypal realm.

And just as there are an infinite number of archetypes, there is no limit to the number of personal symbols we can create for ourselves. When we do something with someone who is special to us, for example, it's not unusual to mark that experience with a trinket that symbolizes the occasion. One woman I know used to take home the matchbooks that restaurants set out for guests. She would write the date and the particular event being celebrated on the inside of the matchbook cover, and then toss the matchbook into an enormous glass bowl she kept on an end table in her living room. It was a lovely idea. Each matchbook held symbolic meaning for her, although absolutely no meaning for anyone else.

Years ago I started bringing home small rocks or stones from places I traveled to that I really loved. The first time I brought a stone home, I wasn't quite sure what to do with it, so I placed it at the base of a large plant in my living room. Over the years, I continued to bring home stones, some that I had collected and others, including beautiful crystals and hand-carved hearts, that were gifts. Eventually a rock garden grew around my favorite plant, symbolizing places and people I loved from all over the world. These stones have absolutely no monetary value, but symbolically they are priceless to me.

We energize our own symbols in life, projecting meaning onto objects, places, and events that are otherwise neutral. A house is just a house until it becomes your home, and then it becomes the container of precious memories, as well as difficult ones. Stones, trinkets, artwork, talismans, good luck charms, and religious icons come to represent the power of protection or good fortune. We cannot stop ourselves from engaging in a ritual of investing objects and places with symbolic meaning, because we have an inherent need to empower the world around us with significance.

Just for fun, next time you go shopping, observe how you make the decision to buy what you buy. You may think that you're heading to the store with a specific item in mind, but unconsciously you are also in the market for refreshing a certain type of power. When you find something you really like, you are drawn to it not just because the size and color and price are right but also because it projects the symbolic message you are shopping for. Does the item say *fun* or *sexy* or *successful* or *slender* or *vibrant*? Does the dress or blouse make you feel good as well as look good? If so, then you've accomplished your goal: you've rebooted your personal feeling of *sexy* or *slender* or *vibrant.* You have found the object that projects exactly the type of power you were looking for.

How many archetypes does a person have?

While you may relate to numerous archetypes in greater and lesser ways, you do not have an endless number of *primary* personal archetypes. Your psyche would implode if that were the case. Rather, you have a cluster of archetypes that are particular to you, forming your Inner-net of influences that express themselves singly and at times blend their energies.

How do we identify our archetypes?

You identify your archetypes in your stories, your patterns, your fears, your talents—all the things that are constant in your nature. What would you say is "typical" of you? How do other people describe you? (If you're up for it, ask your friends for help with this. You would be surprised by what you can learn about yourself.)

Archetypes are patterns in which we know how the story goes. It may be an ancient parable, like the story of David and Goliath, which gave us the archetype of the Bully, or the Damsel in Distress, whose roots go back to the King Arthur legends and to fairy tales like Rapunzel, trapped in her tower waiting for her Rescuer, and Sleeping Beauty awaiting the prince's magic kiss to awaken her. And just as we know these myths and legends, we know our own stories. Some are lovely, some sad, some romantic, some traumatic.

You know what's true about you and always has been true. You know if you are a Rescuer, for example, and if you are, you also know that you will rescue others instinctually, even if you don't want to, because that's how you are wired to respond. Most Rescuers start out rescuing people in return for love, but if at some point, as often happens, your efforts are rejected, then you will finally rescue yourself from your own agenda and go on to help others freely. We can go for years denying our archetypal behavior patterns, but invariably at some point the archetype wins out. Something forces us to confront the pattern, and with that awareness, we reclaim our power.

As you explore the archetypes, you will gain a sense of how they express their characteristic patterns through you, melding the universal, impersonal qualities of the archetype with the specifics of your personality. With practice, you can develop an "archetypal eye," an ability to detach yourself so that you can observe your own patterns of thinking and behavior, and clearly see the myths that you live by.

Another way to discover your archetype is to go the website **www.ArchetypeMe.com** and take the simple and fun quiz.

How can we learn to identify archetypes in other people?

One way to begin identifying archetypes is to look for patterns in popular culture. Princesses populate Disney movies, and Heroes abound in box office blockbusters. But there are plenty of other films in which archetypes are well represented. Miranda Priestly, the lead character in *The Devil Wears Prada*, is a take-charge Queen/Executive if ever there was one; she is said to have been modeled on the iconic *Vogue* editor Anna Wintour. The Advocate turns up in film with regularity; a classic example is the environmental activist Erin Brockovich, in the film of the same name, but there is also Skeeter, the aspiring author in *The Help*, who writes about racism in the South in the 1960s from the perspective of black maids working in white households. Aibileen and Minny, "the help" who dare to tell their stories, are Rebels.

Elsewhere in the culture, we find innovators like Apple's Steve Jobs and Facebook's Mark Zuckerberg, who perfectly embody the Visionary archetype, creating whole new worlds in the most cutting-edge of fields—technology and the Internet. First Ladies like Jacqueline Kennedy, Laura Bush, and Michelle Obama endlessly fascinate us because they represent several powerful archetypes: the Queen, the Caregiver, and the Fashionista. We worship Athletes enough to pay them more than many CEOs and encourage our children to become competitive just like them. Watching LeBron James, Derek Jeter, or the Olympic gymnasts inspires awe because they so perfectly embody their archetype.

You can also look for archetypes closer to home. Is your boss a number-crunching Intellectual or more of a Visionary? Is your child an Athlete or an Artist? How many of your friends are Caregivers and how many are Rebels? What about those next-door neighbors pestering you to compost—are they Devoted Advocates or just aspiring to be green? Observe the archetypes operating in the people you encounter, whether at home, in the workplace, or on the TV screen. And what about the way people present themselves on Facebook? What archetypes might they be communicating intentionally or without even realizing it?

As you become more adept at identifying archetypal patterns in those around you, you will become more comfortable with spotting your own archetypes in action. Do you dream of getting away from it all? That might be your Spiritual Seeker/Mystic archetype calling you to go on retreat. Perhaps you suddenly have the bright idea to go back to school: that's your Intellectual itching to hit the books. And what about the shadow side of your archetypes? Perhaps the Queen in you is butting heads with your equally charismatic King/Boss. Or your children are begging you to stop nagging them, a sure sign the Caregiver in you is turning into a "helicopter" parent.

Do we choose our archetypes? And can we change them?

I love these questions because they suggest that some cosmic force or divine power had something to do with deciding the meaning and purpose of our lives. If we didn't pick out our archetypes, then who did? And even if we did pick them, who organized that opportunity? Was it God? If so, when did that event take place? It would have to have been prior to our birth.

My personal belief is that we are born with life assignments and those assignments are governed by our archetypal patterns. I call these assignments "Sacred Contracts." (That's also the title of a book I wrote, as well as the focus of my teaching.) The archetypes contained in your Sacred Contract govern your relationship to your personal power and to spiritual power, and are expressed through every aspect of your life.

I came to the conclusion about how our archetypes come to us through observation of nature and my deep respect for mystical law. Both nature and mystical law transcend any religion; therefore, their constancy and power is not controlled or organized by any earthly politics or theology. We learn from the laws of nature that life is ordered and ruled by cycles that clearly interact with each other. Nothing exists without a purpose. And we humans are subject to the laws of nature just as everything else on earth is. Our lives were assigned meaning and purpose as part of the order of life itself.

Within these seemingly limitless horizons, however, limits do exist. We are, in a sense, limited by our archetypal makeup. We can only excel at what we are and not at what we would like to be. We are born with a given set of abilities, talents, assets, liabilities, and life challenges in our DNA. This, as some like to say, is the "hand we are dealt." Our archetypal patterns are imprinted in us from birth, perhaps even earlier in the womb. You cannot change your primary archetypes but you can mature their influences. You can transform a Wounded Child into a Magical Child, but the roots of your Wounded Child will always be with you. That is, the wounds of our childhood never leave us, but we can heal their influence upon us. As we mature in life, we have the option of expanding our reach of understanding to include the suffering of other people, including that of our parents. In this way, you are opening yourself to other aspects of the Child archetype beyond the Wounded Child.

To look at this archetypal teaching another way, think of a part of you that you celebrate. Perhaps you love the Entertainer in you or the Healer or the Networker. You just know you're good at this part of your life. You were born good at it. Could you change that? You can't even imagine changing it because it's who you are at the deepest level.

Changing archetypes like items of clothing, then, is not really possible, because you cannot be other than who you really are at your core. Your archetypal patterns are woven through every aspect of your unconscious and conscious nature, from the subtlest levels of your life to the most overt. As you get to know yourself over the years, you come to understand your archetypal patterns and their profound influence upon your psyche. Life brings us opportunities to see ourselves in action: in love, under fire, under stress, in childbirth, acting spontaneously, handling loss, being charitable. We evolve and mature throughout life, but always within our archetypes.

You can pretend to be something other than who you are but eventually you will run out of energy to continue because that's not authentically you. I, for one, have not one shred of the Athlete archetype, and yet that does not stop me from working out at the gym. It does, however, prevent me from pursuing fantasies about competing in the Olympics. While I am certainly free to participate in athletics, my psyche lacks any athletic myth. I can visualize myself running a race, but the vision does not animate my spirit because I do not have the archetype that goes with it. I've met a lot of people who were living a "life on pause" because they had fixated on something for which they were archetypally unsuited. A few of them wanted to be Actors. A few wanted to be Entrepreneurs. One woman fantasized that she was destined to become a great singer-songwriter. None of these individuals had the archetypes required, however, as was reflected in their lack of talent as well as the absence of opportunities coming their way. Opportunities are an extension of your archetypes, and you can only energize opportunities via the archetypes you have.

How do our archetypes work in relationships?

We often speak of "magnetic attraction." We say that we were magnetically attracted to someone from the moment we saw him, and the rest is history. What you are experiencing in a moment like that is a complete animation of an archetype. You feel a buzz inside, a vibration that often moves up the spinal cord and through the skin. This is a full-scale experience of archetypal magnetism. You can barely control your enthusiasm for the person you are connecting with, as the magnetism is literally palpable. If the attraction is romantic, these two people are *Archemates*.

Magnetism is instantaneous. Either it's there or it isn't. And then we have two different experiences of it: magnetic attraction and magnetic connection. Magnetic *attraction* is romantic and magnetic *connection* is the natural network of life—friends, family, and your greater social arena. Both magnetic attractions and magnetic connections vary in intensity. You have necessary connections with some people, nurturing ones with others, and intimate ones with a few. No one can magnetize connections with everyone. Too many, and the result is burnout—being literally and symbolically depleted of energy.

How do our archetypes communicate with us?

Archetypes are not like angels or inner guides. They are not entities with which we have some sort of interactive relationship. It's a common belief that we can communicate with angels and spiritual guides through prayer and that they, in turn, can intervene in our life crises through personal guidance. The operative words here are *personal guidance*. Archetypes are neither responsive to prayer nor do they provide personal guidance. They are impersonal patterns of consciousness that form the essence of human nature. However, archetypes are an active part of our consciousness, continually interacting with the sparks of energy we generate. These cosmic psychic patterns then upgrade old myths into more contemporary dress to keep up with social evolution. For example, we still have the Knight in Shining Armor in our feminine myths and dreams, but his armor today is more likely to consist of an Armani suit and a Mercedes-Benz than a sword and a shield. Myths need to reflect the wardrobe of the times. But take the costume off, and you'll see the same story told over and over again.

One way archetypes communicate with us is by *energizing* or *animating* our myths and fantasies. Some people imagine themselves as Leaders, for example. Abraham Lincoln was one such individual. He knew even in his youth that he was born for some great purpose, and this feeling drove him throughout his childhood to pursue his studies under very difficult conditions and eventually to become a lawyer. But that occupation felt inadequate to him, so he decided to run for political office, as he imagined himself a political Leader. That inner image was animated or energized when Lincoln pictured himself in Congress. Once Lincoln entered politics, he knew he was in alignment with his calling, his life purpose. Not until the Civil War, however, when he faced the challenge of saving the Union, did he realize he was fulfilling the reason for which he was born.

Archetypes can come to us in the form of imagery in our dreams and daydreams. Coincidences and synchronicity also represent archetypal activity. What Carl Jung called synchronicity refers to meaningful coincidences of causally unrelated events. The cosmic forces that organize coincidences and synchronistic happenings intrigued Jung, as it was obvious that some moments in our lives contain such events while others do not. He surmised that we must be participants in some way in the creation of these events through the power of our psyche and archetypal patterns, but no one, not even Jung, has determined the precise alchemical recipe. Still, we view synchronous events as having greater significance than the ordinary events of life, though we are left to discern the meaning of the experiences ourselves—or more accurately, to project a meaning onto them. A childhood friend pops into your mind, someone you haven't thought of in 30 years, and then an hour later, as you're crossing a street, there's the long-forgotten friend coming toward you. It's up to you to make as much or little of this encounter as you choose. But suffice it to say, few of us ignore such happenings, preferring to view them as expressions of archetypal energies spontaneously organizing events in our lives.

What are archetype families?

Archetype families are core groups of archetypes that share a power theme. The Caring family, for example, unites archetypes that express the power of love and nurturing: the Caregiver, the Mother, the Nurturer, the Rescuer, the Teacher. As you will come to appreciate, many archetypes share similar characteristics. Yet although the differences may be subtle, these nuances are significant enough to be represented by separate archetypes. The Companion, for example, is separate from the Sidekick, as the archetype of the Companion suggests a bond of emotional devotion whereas the Sidekick is a playmate.

It is not possible to explore every well-known archetype within the pages of this book, but by clustering many of them into archetype families, we can give you a sense of the core power structure of archetypes. You may find that you resonate more with an archetype family as a whole than with any individual archetype. This is not unusual. (For descriptions of some archetypes other than the ten we profiled, see the Archetype Gallery on page 235.)

Why is learning about archetypes so useful?

While you may begin investigating your archetypes on a lark—as a fun, "more about me" adventure—the hidden power of exploring your archetypes is precisely that it *is* "more about you," only in this case, the *real* you. None of us begins life knowing who we are or why we're the way we are. We have to search deeply for that knowledge. Once that first stirring of curiosity about yourself is triggered, you initiate a quest for inner knowledge: *Who am I? What is my purpose? What is the nature of my inner power?* These are not ordinary questions, and they are not answered by finding the right job or the right lover. These are cries from the depth of your being, calling you to discover your true self, who longs to be embraced without hesitation or fear. Your archetypes hold the imprint of that true self.

A woman once told me, "I need to go away and find my Self." I knew when she said it that she didn't mean "find *myself*," but "my *Self*," with a capital *S*. She had awakened to her inner nature, to that part of her that was more than her personality, more than her daily routines. She had discovered the inner voice that is separate from the ordinary self that organized her life by rules and expectations.

I asked her, "What do you think you'll find on this quest for your inner Self?"

"I have always wanted to be an artist," she said. "I know I am an artist. I have never given my Self a chance to do my art because I told 'myself' that no one took me seriously, so how could I take me seriously? But I feel as if I am living a false life, a lie. I can't stand it anymore. I don't care if I starve. I would rather live a hungry authentic life than an abundant lie."

In meeting her Self, this woman had encountered her Artist archetype. She could no longer continue to live a life of self-betrayal, blaming others for her choice not to fulfill her archetypal destiny.

In what other ways can knowing about our archetypes help us?

In working with thousands of people over the years, as both a teacher and a medical intuitive, I've come to believe that an examination of your myths is as essential to good health as an examination of your body. Disappointments, heartaches, and life crises that are the result of your life plans are difficult to heal, not just because of whatever logistical messes result but also because your myths were shattered. Indeed, sometimes it's easier to recover from a physical crisis than from a myth crisis. It can be difficult to heal from a myth crisis if you don't even realize you're in one! An unacknowledged myth crisis can be the seed of lifelong depression and even a terminal illness.

"I've always pictured myself married with two children and living by the sea," a woman told me. When she was 25, she married a young lawyer, and the couple moved to Cape Cod. Six years and two kids later, her husband was staying later and later at the office. You know the story, and so did her intuition, but she could not bring herself to admit the truth. It was a diagnosis of colon cancer that finally compelled her to "vomit out the truth," as she put it, after swallowing the lies for years.

She came to see me because she wanted to understand more about why she had become ill and why she wasn't healing. By then, she was no longer married and no longer living by the sea. I told her that we needed to discuss her "perfect marriage myth" gone wrong. What myth did she now have as a replacement?

Infuriated, she told me, "I still want to be married with two kids, living by the sea. I will not give that up. I will not! He cannot take that dream"—that is, myth—"away from me!"

But events had already taken that myth away from her. She was divorced, ill, and undergoing chemotherapy. But which was really destroying this woman—her cancer or the shattering of her myth? What she needed in order to heal was a new, more appropriate myth that would give her a reason to live.

Discovering your archetypes is like being introduced to yourself at the soul level. You may not know yourself at this depth, or the power that your myths and symbols generate in your life. But you should, because these are the creative engines of your psyche and spirit. And knowing them can save your life.

How can we awaken to the truth of our archetypes without getting ill?

Awakening to the truth of your archetype is about becoming more responsible and taking care of your own needs, both external and internal. You need to learn to recognize and interpret that language that you are most responsive to at a deeper level, which is the language of your own symbols and myths.

People today are becoming more self-aware, exploring the inner Self through therapy and counseling, as well as meditation and spirituality. We have awakened our intuition. We now require different tools of consciousness through which to navigate our lives, and one of the basic tools is understanding who we are and how we function at the archetypal level.

How can knowing about archetypes help us through life transitions?

Not only do we have archetypes that connect us with our personal myths, fantasies, and ideas about our world, but life itself is also governed by archetypal experiences that are common to us all. Among them is the cycle of death and rebirth—the universal experience of shedding one form in order to create another. This is represented by the myth of the phoenix, the bird that is consumed in flames and then reborn from the ashes.

We all go through passages in which we come to a crossroads, a choice point, and the direction of our life shifts dramatically by virtue of a decision we make. In the same way, we can experience archetypal transitions, a shift from the authority of one or more dominant archetypes in our complex of archetypes to another archetype. "Empty-nest syndrome" can trigger just such an archetypal transition. Stay-at-home Mothers in particular experience this. After devoting years to caring for their children, once the children leave home, the archetypal Mother role that has dominated their being evaporates. Farsighted stay-at-home Moms prepare for this transition by rebooting their careers or going back to school or finding other interests not related to child rearing. These women transition smoothly into their next phase, frequently with great excitement about entering a whole new chapter of their life. But if you don't prepare for the next archetypal chapter in life you will transition into a crisis zone. You will feel as if you've lost a part of your identity, as indeed you have.

I've seen this happen to married people who have lost a spouse and are transitioning into widowhood. When the death occurs in the later years or after a prolonged illness, the surviving spouse has the benefit of a period of adjusting to the inevitable loss of the partner. But when the death is unexpected, perhaps through an accident or a heart attack or a stroke, the surviving spouse is thrust into limbo. Having woken up a wife, she goes to bed that night a widow. Instantly removed from her familiar mythological landscape, the surviving spouse must now find a new myth for a new future. Some people find it nearly impossible to shed the old myth and move on, choosing instead to remain in mourning, connected to the shadow of the old myth—to its sadness. By holding on to this pain and even nurturing it, the widow postpones the life-changing transition of widowhood and remains connected to the idea of being married.

Of course, we also experience glorious transitions throughout life, some of which include falling in love, becoming parents, and awakening to the power of the inner Self. Life is an archetypal magic carpet ride through endless adventures meant to teach us about the hidden truths of life and our place in the cosmic scheme.

How to Use This Book

I have designed this book to walk you through the archetypes in detail so that you can begin to identify which ones are operative in your own life and in the lives of those around you. Learning about archetypes will enable you to connect fully with their power and forge an intimate connection with yourself as well as develop a deeper understanding of other people. Even if you relate immediately to a particular archetype, there is still a great deal to gain by reading all the chapters. Much of the fun of knowing about archetypes is being able to spot them in your daily life. As you observe people, you'll find yourself automatically thinking things like "Oh, he's obviously an Intellectual," or "That's a very Queen-like thing to do."

Each of the following chapters is devoted to a single archetype. No one archetype is more important than any other: they're arranged in alphabetical order. Each profile is divided into topics that will help clarify its meaning:

Life Journey: This section describes in detail the features and behavior patterns typically associated with that particular archetype.

Unique Challenge: This sets out issues or challenges that emerge naturally out of the characteristics of the archetype. For example, some archetypes—the Caretaker, for one—are inherently passive or receptive when it comes to love, while others, like the Lover, are more likely to take the initiative. The Unique Challenge involves coming to know *what* forces are driving an archetype as they express themselves through an individual's personality.

Universal Lesson: Each archetype contains a life lesson, or soul lesson, that is key to the inner development of individuals with that archetype.

Defining Grace: Each archetype is also endowed with a particular grace, or mystical force that empowers the individual and supports personal growth.

Inner Shadow: All archetypes have characteristics that operate "in shadow"—outside of our conscious awareness.

Through confronting these unconscious shadow aspects we uncover our fears and negative behavior patterns, a step toward releasing them.

Male Counterpart: This section describes ways in which an archetype expresses itself uniquely in men.

Myths: Myths are the signature stories associated with an archetype, the narrative through which its deeper symbolic meaning is conveyed.

Recognize Your Archetype: This section summarizes the characteristics and behavior patterns of an archetype to help you determine whether or not it is "your" archetype—a defining force in your life.

Lifestyle Challenge: This refers to challenges arising from *how* an archetype introduces its particular patterns of influence into an individual's life. These influences may express themselves psychologically or creatively or through personal habits and rituals.

Step into Your Archetype: Each chapter closes with a series of exercises to help you tap into the power of the archetype.

As you go through the book, it's important to keep in mind that archetypes are creatures of the psyche. They are not literal, but mystical. Archetypes are impossible to define with precision because archetypal patterns morph to fit each individual. Two people may have the Caregiver archetype but the manner in which the archetype expresses itself will differ according to the contours and demands of each person's life. Once you learn to identify an archetypal pattern, however, you will be able to look at your own life or someone else's and see the subtle ways in which the archetype influences that life. Archetypes may be impossible to define, yet they are always recognizable.

Once you connect with an archetype that you know is genuinely you, it will inspire you to find out about other archetypes that may be influencing your life. Connecting with an archetype is a bridge to your true Self, to who you really are.

You are far more than your personality, more than your habits, more than your achievements. You are an infinitely complex human being with stories and myths and dreams—and ambitions of cosmic proportions. Don't waste time underestimating yourself. Dream big. Use your archetypes. If you're an Artist, make art. If you're a Visionary, imagine something the future needs, then join forces with an Entrepreneur to make a venture out of it. Use the energy of your archetype to express the true reason you were born. Life was never meant to be safe. It was meant to be lived right to the end.

There are inner riches awaiting you in the archetypal domain. Turn the page and dive in!

CHAPTER 3

The Advocate

Archetype Family: *Advocate*

Other Expressions: *Organo, Naturist, Defender*

Life Journey: *To be a conscious agent for positive social/environmental change*

Unique Challenge: *To find a cause that engages your strength and talent rather than your anger or personal agenda*

Universal Lesson: *Just because you can't do everything should not stop you from doing something.*

Defining Grace: *Hope*

Inner Shadow: *Believing that others must appreciate the value of your work. Believing that your work has more purpose than what others do.*

Male Counterpart: *Advocate, Social Rights Activist, Health Soldier*

Myth of the Advocate: *Forcing change*

Behavior Patterns and Characteristics: *The Advocate . . .*

- *is dedicated to social, political, and environmental transformation.*
- *is committed to advancing humanitarian causes.*
- *speaks out for those who have no voice.*
- *fights for human rights and environmental protection.*

Lifestyle Challenge: *How will a commitment to a cause change my lifestyle?*

Life Journey

The Advocate may be the most unfamiliar archetype among our family of ten. That's because this is a relatively recent addition to the cosmic theater, having emerged as a recognized pattern of power with the rise of civil consciousness and social action in the 1960s. Advocates are dedicated to advancing humanitarian concerns for the benefit of society, championing the rights of those who can't speak up for themselves. The goal of this archetype is no less than social, political, and environmental transformation. People with the Advocate archetype are magnets for social underdogs. Individuals or groups that lack the clout to represent their needs through social, political, or financial channels find in the Advocate someone to carry the charge for them.

Advocates seldom have to think twice about whether they are Advocates. This particular archetype has a GPS that homes in with particular zeal on whatever needs to be changed in the world. As an Advocate, you are drawn to social concerns because you were born to make a difference, to improve life for others in some way. The term *change agent*—often used to describe the Advocate—is an impulse that courses through this archetype in varying degrees of intensity. Change is not something we humans welcome with open arms; a reluctance to let go of the familiar seems to be built into our DNA. But the underlying momentum of change always has its way, tearing down the old and providing opportunities to build new structures. The Life Journey of the Advocate is intimately woven into the natural law of change.

As an Advocate you have a fire in the belly that is automatically ignited when you see a way to make a difference in the world. This is an archetype that gives its all so that the lives of others will improve. If the label *Advocate* is relatively new, the impetus to take action on behalf of the downtrodden is not. The forerunners of the Advocate go back centuries. Among the most renowned are the abolitionists who fought to eliminate slavery in America before the Civil War, the committees that championed reform of child labor in the 19th and early 20th centuries, and the suffragettes who bravely fought for a woman's right to vote. These and other groups laid the groundwork and sturdy wiring for the rise of social advocacy and activism that erupted in the civil rights movement of the 1960s, which gave birth to a new era of social freedoms, and the antiwar movement, which helped end U.S. involvement in the Vietnam War. As the window of opportunity for social and political change opened wide, the environmental and feminist movements began to take shape. Without the Advocate archetype and its formidable predecessors, the social and sexual freedoms we now take for granted would not be a part of our lives. Threats to some of these freedoms today are prompting a new generation of Advocates and their Rebel cousins to take up the charge.

Common occupations for the Advocate include lawyer, social worker, environmentalist, philanthropist, community organizer, writer, and media professional. You can also be effective in business if you have the Visionary or Entrepreneur archetype as well. Advocates with the Rebel archetype may take to the streets and demonstrate for a cause. Without a doubt, movements such as PETA (People for the Ethical Treatment of Animals) and MADD (Mothers Against Drunk Driving) were initiated by Advocates and Rebels.

Advocates are often effective public speakers, but you don't just talk a good game. This is an archetype with an activist edge, concerned with righting systems that are headed in the wrong direction. Many of you are drawn to the power-and-justice end of the spectrum, dedicating your energies to fighting against human rights violations or the endless stream of ecological disasters that could be avoided with more conscious laws governing our relationship with nature. Other Advocates express the archetype through initiating projects like urban gardens and recycling, inspiring people to live more consciously. Regardless of what form the Advocate's activism takes, this archetype has an agenda, and that agenda is to foster positive change and initiate new beginnings. Your Life Journey as an Advocate is to be an agent for societal transformation.

But if the Life Journey is the same for all Advocates, not every individual with the archetype is the same. In each Advocate, archetypal characteristics commingle with the ingredients of the individual's personality to produce an Advocate like no other. Still, a glance at the archetype as a whole suggests that most Advocates fall into one of three categories:

The Hobby Advocate

The Hobby Advocate is someone who wants to do something worthwhile but hasn't yet connected with a way to make a difference, at least if a long-term or open-ended commitment is involved. Not that Hobby Advocates are dilettantes. Far from it. If you are a Hobby Advocate, you're among the primary carriers of social-mindedness and form the base of much community activity. Usually Hobby Advocates look for a clearly delineated timeline before committing to a project. You also look for projects that are noncontroversial. You're not an activist, preferring to focus on improving your community rather than working toward radical social or political change. You might advocate for a neighborhood garden or a day-care center, organize a farmers' market, sponsor anti-bullying measures, lobby schools for healthier lunches, or raise money to fund summer programs for kids. You're just learning the ropes, so your primary concern is not tackling larger issues of social injustice or fighting environmental crimes.

The Devoted Advocate

The Devoted Advocate has taken advocacy to the next level and beyond. The Devoted Advocate is exactly what the name suggests: someone who has carefully chosen a path of long-term commitment to social, environmental, humanitarian, political, or economic change, and has willingly assumed the personal and financial risks of making such a pledge. People who advocate green living, for example, are not living green for a weekend. For you, adopting an organic lifestyle involves building a small solar home or retrofitting an existing house, planting an organic garden, recycling wastes, wearing recycled clothing, driving a hybrid car or using public transportation, as well as working to raise consciousness of green living and lobbying for legislative change. Dedicated to a sustainable lifestyle, green-living people—*organos,* as we call them—are truly pioneers. You've gone ahead of the rest of us to lay the groundwork for what will one day be commonplace for all conscious people.

Yet another expression of the Devoted Advocate is the person who strives to save historic sites. It's amazing how many people walk by monumental buildings and historical sites that are absolute treasures and don't even notice them, or have no idea of the value of the architecture that makes up the beauty of their town or city. Jacqueline Kennedy Onassis was instrumental in the preservation of some of America's most important buildings, beginning with the restoration of the White House when she was First Lady and later with the preservation of New York City landmarks like Grand Central Station. History and architecture Advocates lobby local and state legislatures to landmark important sites and work to restore them to their former glory for posterity. These Devoted Advocates are responsible for saving some of the most precious work of our ancestors, and because of their efforts, our towns and cities are vibrant and full of architectural diversity, rather than cold and starkly modern.

The Compulsive Advocate

The Compulsive Advocate is in some ways the most vulnerable of the three expressions of the Advocate archetype. The Compulsive Advocate is often motivated to participate in social causes because such activities fill a personal emotional need. Groups sponsoring social change generally have a lot of positive energy swirling around them, and doing good for others is very energizing, inspiring the people involved to say things like "I've never felt more alive than when I was helping people." For the Compulsive Advocate, the emotional high of committing to a cause and associating with enthusiastic Advocate companions can be very addictive. The social camaraderie becomes more important than the cause itself. What eventually happens, however, is that the investment of time and energy starts to feel more like confinement than commitment, and the Compulsive Advocate's interest wanes. Then, as an excuse to pull away, the Compulsive Advocate may become very critical of the cause, questioning the purpose or the policies or even the integrity of the organization. Once Compulsive Advocates are free, however, their need to get their social adrenaline pumping again inevitably leads them to seek out another cause. This cycle may be repeated endlessly. It's not that Compulsive Advocates are insincere; most are genuinely seeking a cause they can really get behind. But because they are primarily motivated by emotional needs rather than altruistic passion, they find commitment to any cause too challenging.

Of course, there are Advocates who don't fit neatly into any category, and no Advocate is consigned to a category forever. Often, Hobby Advocates who have gotten a taste of community activity are drawn to deepen their commitment to an organization or issue. Similarly, a Compulsive Advocate may tire of flitting from one group to another looking for social connection and become motivated to pick a cause and make a serious commitment to it.

Unique Challenge

Advocates face many challenges, because this archetype is genetically programmed to identify what needs to be changed in the world. You home in on what's wrong in society, what needs fixing, what could be done better, and who is hurting. Taken together, the ills of society comprise a pretty long list of conditions that most people don't want to think about. As an Advocate, however, you have an innate passion for wanting to right things that are wrong. Your purpose in life is to make society a better and more humane place. This passion is your greatest asset, but like all assets, it must be handled skillfully or it can become a liability. Passion mixed with wisdom, talent, and an abundance of hope generally creates an undefeatable alchemy of the soul. But to be an effective Advocate, you need to be realistic about human nature and the consciousness of society when you step in and try to change things. Striving to make the world into some kind of utopian ideal would be as futile a goal as trying to swim across the Atlantic to Europe. That's not to say you shouldn't swim at all, just that you shouldn't embark on a swim that's guaranteed to fail. Similarly, in setting out to make social change, it's essential to have realistic goals. Don't choose a goal that will exhaust your resources or make you angry if you can't meet it.

For an Advocate, knowing your own strengths and weaknesses and realistically assessing your goals are the keys to determining where you should and should not invest your time and energy. Without that type of clarity, even as a Hobby Advocate you run the risk of ending up feeling frustrated or useless. Even worse, you could be attracted to a cause because of your anger or unhealed wounds. Joining Mothers Against Drunk Driving because of painful events that occurred in your own alcoholic family might seem appropriate and even emotionally healing, but unless you can transcend your personal issues for the sake of the group's agenda, your pain will find a way of expressing itself—probably passive-aggressively—that will serve neither you nor the cause. It's always smart to check whether you are drawn to a cause for its own sake or because you are seeking a witness to your own grief or unfinished business.

Advocacy groups are not support groups. So to be effective as an Advocate, you must use discernment in deciding where your talents and limitations are a fit. It is not your anger that will help people but your vision and inspiration.

Universal Lesson

Sadly, the world will never run out of problems that need solutions, crises that need remedies, and people who need help. The prospect can be overwhelming. We are left with the agonizing feeling of *What can I possibly do?* If we were watching Rome burn with only a cup of water in our hands, the logical answer would be, "Drink and run, because all is lost." But we're not watching Rome burn, and logic is not your best friend when it comes to considering whether or not to get involved. You can always talk yourself into believing that small efforts don't matter when weighed against great challenges. History, however, tells a different story. It's full of small actions with big results, in which one person's courageous stand transformed the world. Remember Rosa Parks, the African-American woman who refused to give up her seat on the bus to a white person? "I was tired of giving in," was her explanation later on. In that small but daring action, which gave impetus to the civil rights movement, Parks perfectly expressed the essence of the Advocate archetype.

For an Advocate, engaging in some form of social action is inevitable. You don't have to set the world on fire, though many with this archetype were born with the talent to do just that. The lesson of the Advocate is to accept that just because you can't do everything doesn't mean you can't do something. Be directed by what you *can* do, rather than stopped by what you can't.

Defining Grace: Hope

If only one grace were to be granted to humanity, I would choose the grace of hope, for while all the graces are magnificent, hope is essential. Life without hope is nearly impossible to endure, but with hope the impossible is surmountable. Hope is the grace most appropriate for the Advocate archetype, since people devoted to forging new paths for humanity keep hope alive for others through their actions. Advocates inspire the rest of us to invest in worthy or necessary causes in order to make the world a better place, and in doing so, they renew hope in our hearts again and again.

Whether an Advocate is battling for human rights or working to raise ecological awareness or implementing sustainable business plans, the fact is, the wheels of change turn slowly when attempting to introduce new ways of thinking, especially if the new threatens the old. If not for the grace of hope—hope for a better tomorrow, hope that new ideas will produce new outcomes, hope that caring about the needs of other human beings matters—what would have the power to keep a true Advocate going?

Hope is the one grace that has sustained humanity through the darkest times. In the classic Greek myth, when Pandora disobeyed orders and opened the jar that Zeus gave her, she released all the evils into the world. But one thing remained in the bottom of the jar—hope.

Hope is what fills your heart with the knowledge that you will make it through bleak times, that all difficulties inevitably come to an end. Hope sustains the Advocate with truisms like *Every day is a new beginning* and *Your life can change in the blink of an eye.* Hope is what keeps you believing in miracles, even if you have never experienced one. Above all, hope is the grace you hold on to fiercely when you or a loved one or society at large is in need of healing. Perhaps no one realizes how real and powerful the grace of hope can be more than the Advocate who carries on in spite of every indication that the cause is lost.

Inner Shadow

All the Advocate's good intentions—and they are many—contain the potential for becoming negative. Because Advocates are so passionate and so personally invested in the social, political, or environmental causes they espouse, they are especially vulnerable to the need for appreciation for their dedication.

It is a formidable task to commit yourself, like the Devoted Advocate described earlier, to a lifestyle in which everything you do, wear, eat, drive, and think is in harmony with a green-living philosophy. As an Advocate of such a lifestyle, you must read the labels on all products, buy or grow only organic food (or go hungry if you can't find any), drive a hybrid car or bicycle everywhere—the list goes on. It's easy to see how an Advocate pouring such effort into "conscious" living could be judgmental of those not making half that effort to care for the environment.

The same can be said of the Devoted Human Rights Advocate or any other expression of this archetype in which the Advocate has committed heart and soul. There are risks involved in committing to a cause, including wanting others to understand the importance of your cause as passionately as you do. Sometimes the people you meet are in denial about the issues. Other times, the issues that are yours to deal with are not theirs. They may be called to help move society along in other ways, if not today then perhaps tomorrow.

But this is the shadow side of being an Advocate. Regardless of the sacrifices you make in behalf of your cause, you must always bear in mind that you lead best by example. There is always something more you can do—and there will always be people who see only what you *haven't* done, and they can't or won't express appreciation for your efforts. To give critics the benefit of the doubt, remember that many people who are not Advocates have no clue what kind of personal sacrifices and risks you undertake in order to make their world a better place. Sometimes all you can do is forgive them for their ignorance.

The other side of the Advocate's shadow is a kind of superiority that says, "What I'm doing has so much more purpose than whatever you're doing." This attitude can be poisonous, separating you from the very people you are devoting your life to helping. Try to remember that everyone, everywhere, is doing the best they can. It may not come up to your standards, but just as you don't like being reminded of what you haven't accomplished, others don't like being told their efforts are worth nothing.

Male Counterpart

The male Advocate shares all the same attributes as the female, as well as the same challenges. In terms of effectiveness as Advocates, gender matters not at all. There are some differences, however, in how Advocate males choose to express their archetype. One expression today is the organic farmer, who is struggling to keep his farm clean from the genetically modified organism (GMO) seeds forced on him through corporate channels. These Advocates for healthy seeds in healthy soil are rapidly evolving as "Health Soldiers," in the fight to ensure better health for all. The struggle to maintain chemical-free seeds has spread across the world, and many of these Advocates are warehousing wholesome seeds as they become rare commodities on this planet. Their commitment goes hand in hand with the growing consumer demand for heirloom tomatoes and other vegetables grown from non-GMO seeds.

Two other male expressions of the Advocate are the Environmentalist and the Social Rights Activist. Men with these archetypes are often found in organizations like Doctors Without Borders, World Vets (a kind of "veterinarians without borders"), and the United Nations Volunteers, offering their skills in high-risk areas and third world countries. Though women Advocates are also devoting their lives to concerns like these, male Advocates in particular gravitate to organizations involved with community development and nation building, disaster relief, construction, and applied technology, as well as social justice and environmental initiatives and conservation.

Myth of the Advocate

The myth of the Advocate is the idea that we can make people change or make them see the value of the work we're doing. However, wisdom teaches us that the more we push, the more the opposition holds their ground. None of us likes having anything forced down our throats. The Advocate has to be sharp, clever, patient, wise, and creative to be heard. Whenever you are introducing change into a family, an institution, an economy, or a society, you can be sure that it will be a threat to someone—if only because they recognize the power in the message you bring.

Advocates for alternative energy, for example, continually face political and economic battles. And yet, though they appear to lose more battles than they win, it's inevitable that they will win the energy war, because eventually the planet will run out of fossil fuels. Advocates encouraging entrepreneurs to invest in a solar-based energy future will not have marched in vain. It's just a matter of time before change will not be a matter of choice.

For the Advocate facing a lonely and uphill battle, there is only one course of action: *Believe in your message.* Believe in your ability to go the distance. And let go of the need to seek the approval of others.

Lifestyle Challenge

There is a reason why people are commitment phobic in our society: commitments change your life. They represent an investment of your time, energy, attention, and funds that by definition requires you to reorder your priorities. In other words, commitments take time away from *you.* To the question *Will a commitment to a cause change my lifestyle?* the simple answer is yes. But to the question *How will it change it?* the answer is that much will depend on your individual circumstances. But one thing is sure: your life will no longer be about just you. If you are serious about advocacy, the central focus and driver of your life will be the cause to which you pledge your time and energy—and possibly your material resources.

We never used to be a commitment-phobic society. For much of history, meeting someone unable to make a commitment was practically unheard of. Then came the 1970s, the "Me Decade," when the concern for political and social justice that characterized the 1960s gave way to an obsession with self-actualization and personal well-being.

Since then our fundamental way of interacting with life itself has shifted. Technology and the Internet have converted our lives into a vast network of energy relationships. Now we measure our value according to our personal energy, and our decisions about whether to make a commitment to a project or relationship are based more on how much personal energy it will demand than on factors like our skills and resources or even the significance of the project. If a project—or relationship—will require too much of our energy, we hesitate before making a commitment to it or walk away altogether.

As a society we have collectively shifted our emphasis from activities that are community and family oriented—and thus commitment centered—to those that emphasize personal interests, self-development, and making money. Few people want to venture out of their comfort zone if it means learning about what isn't working in our world and needs to be changed or, heaven forbid, how their own lifestyle is contributing to environmental degradation.

The dominant values today present their own unique challenges because they have allowed us to believe that life is "all about me." But it's not, and it never has been. Life is about what we can do for others. And if you have the Advocate active in your psyche, then you were born to be a participant in the dynamic time in which we're now living, as it challenges us on every front to make significant social, political, and environmental changes.

Recognize Your Archetype:
Are You an Advocate?

If you have the Advocate archetype it is very hard not to know it, as you are almost certainly involved in some kind of social or environmental or political action, or thinking about it at any rate. But let's say you've been caught up in some other archetype in your makeup—raising a family perhaps, if you have the Caregiver in you, or studying, if your Intellectual has been earning a degree.

But now you feel a stirring of desire to do something positive in the world, to make a contribution. Is there enough of the Advocate in you to take the next step and actually get involved? Take a look at the behavior patterns and characteristics of the Advocate on the next page and see if you resonate with them.

BEHAVIOR PATTERNS AND CHARACTERISTICS OF
THE ADVOCATE

- You are naturally drawn to social, political, or environmental concerns.

- You feel a need to make a difference in the world.

- You are committed to doing something worthwhile with your life.

- You are dedicated to fixing what isn't working in society.

- You are moved to take action when you see or hear about the mistreatment of people or animals or the environment.

- You see a problem, and you immediately start thinking of ways to solve it.

- You are drawn to the plight of a particular group or cause.

- You work in an activist field like law, social work, health care, or community development, or you are considering making it your career.

- Your response to news of natural disasters or other major crises is to think how you could help those involved.

- You admire celebrities who go to troubled hotspots to offer humanitarian aid or bring the issue to the attention of the world community.

- You speak out for those who have no voice.

- You are committed to advancing humanitarian causes.

Step into Your Archetype: Tapping into the Power of the Advocate

The challenge for an Advocate is managing your commitment. Toward that end, some of the following actions could help you find the place where your energy and skills would be most effective.

- **Think globally, act locally.** It's fine to envision sweeping change, but when it comes to getting something accomplished, tackling too big a problem on too large a scale is a setup for frustration and failure. Start small, in your local area or with an issue that's familiar, and keep your initial involvement modest. Success comes with incremental progress. Build credibility as you give yourself a chance to learn.

- **Network.** Nowhere is it more obvious that we need one another than in activist work. Advocacy is a team endeavor. One Advocate can cast the net but it takes many more to haul in the catch. As we saw from recent presidential elections and the Occupy movement, the synergy can be phenomenal when you make optimal use of social networking. But don't forget old-fashioned offline communication, too. If you're raising money, making a pitch face to face is often the most effective way to get someone to write a check or get involved.

- **Do your research.** While you're casting about for a cause to commit to, listen to your gut. What issue would you like to see resolved? Is there an area that moves you—health, say, or women's issues or animal rights? Is there a geographical area you're drawn to—Darfur, perhaps, or Haiti or Appalachia? What skills do you have to apply toward solving a problem? You may not be a doctor or development expert but perhaps you have a PR or accounting background, tech savvy, or a way with people or words—all highly marketable in the Advocacy world. Once you've narrowed your sights to a few organizations, check them out on a website like Charity Navigator that rates nonprofits on factors like management and use of funding. Good Advocates invest their time and energy wisely.

- **Be a NIMBY buster.** Nobody, it seems, wants a halfway house or homeless shelter in their neighborhood. Hence the acronym NIMBY (Not In My Back Yard). But humanitarian services have to go somewhere, and not all are as undesirable neighbors as the people who oppose them believe. If you have strong diplomatic skills coupled with an Advocate archetype, you may be just the person to bring about social change so that everyone wins.

- **Hobby, Devoted, or Compulsive?** Flip back to the Life Journey section and see which Advocate category fits you best. You can avoid disappointment if you're clear about the level of commitment you're capable of *now*—not next year—and whether your expectations are realistic. A Hobby Advocate can get away with the odd Sunday handing out flyers, but if you sign on to play a key role in a political campaign, be prepared for long nights at work and weeks on the road. Can you afford it financially and emotionally? Will your family suffer as a result of your involvement?

- **Fire in the belly or conflagration?** Passion is an Advocate's best asset, and it's natural to be motivated by frustration at injustice or widespread neglect. But you won't help and could harm if you let a personal grudge fuel your advocacy. Before you sign on, douse any fires of rage and make sure your focus is on the group's agenda and not a personal one.

- **Be your own best advocate.** Caring archetypes can lose power if you don't take care of yourself. Remember the basics: eat right, exercise, moderation in all. You need to be in fighting trim to fight for others' rights.

- **Save the world.** With the Internet, it's never been easier to find a cause to commit to anywhere on the globe. Clearing houses like the Global Volunteer Network will link you to opportunities in every conceivable region and field. If you're still casting about for your calling, you can commit to a cause for as little as a week before you dive in long term.

To the Advocate, power is all-important. It's the fuel you need to do your work in the world. Much of your power comes from speaking out for those who have no voice. And here are some other ways your archetype can gain power—or regain it if you lose it.

Where You Gain Power

- **Being clear about your motivation.** The desire to change others' lives for the better is good, but self-interest is a power killer.

- **Knowing your subject.** Passion is not enough. Learn all you can about your advocacy area.

- **Being patient.** Change happens at its own pace. You can't force it.

- **Being a team player.** Even Joan of Arc had an army behind her.

- **Staying hopeful.** You must believe in what you're doing to keep going when the going is tough.

Where You Lose Power (and how to regain it)

- **Being in it for the wrong reasons.** Advocacy work isn't a social club. Focus on your organization's goals.

- **Being a missionary, not an advocate.** You're not trying to convert the natives but to inspire change. You'll win more support with a well-conceived, well-executed campaign.

- **Being unrealistic.** Despair happens when you aim too high. Let go of expectations and just do your best, a step at a time.

- **Craving recognition.** Maybe your work will be acknowledged, maybe not. Either way, keep moving toward your goal.

- **Being competitive.** Don't try to out-advocate others. Value your own contribution.

Checklist for the Advocate

☐ I'm committed to doing my best for the cause.

☐ I value everyone's contributions, not just my own.

☐ I realize Rome wasn't built in a day, and I'm willing to put in the time.

☐ If I feel myself getting riled up, I'll back away until I can act with a calm, clear mind.

☐ I keep abreast of what other activists are doing, so we can work together for a common cause.

Final Thoughts

There has never been a time in history so primed for the talents of true Advocates. Listen to your heart, find your cause, and commit to it.

CHAPTER 4

The Artist/Creative

Archetype Family: *Creative*

Other Expressions: *Performer, Storyteller*

Life Journey: *To cultivate the imagination and explore new forms of creative expression*

Unique Challenge: *To overcome the fear of not being original*

Universal Lesson: *To not diminish or ignore your talent but instead to develop your unique artistic gifts*

Defining Grace: *Creativity*

Inner Shadow: *Fear of being ordinary or unacknowledged for your artistic gifts, or resentful that you chose not to develop your inner Artist/Creative*

Male Counterpart: *The Artist/ Creative is a yin/yang archetype, balancing masculine and feminine energies.*

Myths of the Artist/ Creative: *I will never be able to support myself if I pursue a career in the arts. Artist/Creatives are temperamental and eccentric, and lead counterculture lives. Substance abuse is a risk of the creative life.*

Behavior Patterns and Characteristics: *The Artist/ Creative . . .*

- *sees beauty everywhere.*
- *comes alive in front of an audience.*
- *plays music or appreciates it.*
- *dreams of seeing her name on the bestseller list.*
- *can't wait to find her art form.*
- *commits wholeheartedly to realizing her creative dreams.*

Lifestyle Challenge: *Can I develop my talent and express myself, or will fear of failure or humiliation hold me back?*

Life Journey

The Artist/Creative is one of the most intriguing archetypes because of its profound contribution to the evolution of the human psyche and the many ways in which it expresses itself. The Artist/Creative's journey is one of imagining, interpreting, and giving form to what the ordinary eye cannot see. In all its expressions—artist, performer, storyteller, creator—the Artist/Creative archetype pulsates with a need to reveal the many colors in the spectrum of life, to illustrate the countless forms in which nature presents itself, and to capture beauty in all its manifestations. Beauty is a magnet for the Artist—creating beauty, as well as finding beauty in the ordinary. We love the arts precisely because they have the power to transform the mundane into the enchanting, the commonplace into the spectacular.

Many people associate the word *artist* with Visual Artists, particularly painters and sculptors. As a Visual Artist, your raison d'être is to communicate in two or three dimensions your richly textured, many-layered vision of the world. Today's Visual Artist has a multitude of expressive channels available, from painting, sculpture, and drawing to printmaking, graphic design, crafts, photography, and film. Without a doubt, the high-tech domain has also opened a portal to dimensions of visual creativity that were unimaginable prior to such technology.

The Visual Artist comes from the longest line of symbolic expression. Before there was written language, people relied on visual language, telling their stories through drawings and paintings, first on the walls of caves and later on parchment, canvas, and other materials. Talented artists depicted their gods and heroes in marble and set out Bible stories in stained glass windows and illuminated manuscripts. Visual Artists became masters at blending art and symbol to communicate hidden codes of power. The influence of the Visual Artist is unparalleled in its impact on the evolution of our social and spiritual soul, yet this is just one expression of the Artist/Creative archetype.

The Performer is another important expression of this archetype, revealed primarily through theater, music, dance, and drama.

If you have the Performer in you, you experience it as a passion, even a calling, to share your inner experience of the world through your particular art form. Performers long to ignite in their audience the same fire they feel for whatever they are playing or portraying. Actors in particular say they come alive when they feel a connection with their audience. As a Performer you need, even crave, this connection as a validation of what is extraordinary about your performance and your talent. When there is not that give-and-take between Performer and audience, the performance suffers. A Performer who has perfected her craft is said to have attained the stature of an artist of the stage.

Like many archetypes, the Performer often appears early in life. A man I know who is a professional dancer in Broadway productions—and in his off hours takes creative improvisation classes—told me that he was "dancing in his diapers." In school, he could hardly keep his feet still, as he mentally executed dance steps instead of paying attention to the lessons. The moment he walked onstage in his first high school production he knew this was where he belonged—and where he would be for the rest of his life. It's a familiar story. Archetypal patterns run deep in us. They embody what we know to be true about ourselves, in some cases almost from birth.

Beyond the outward expressions of the Artist/Creative is a more intimate understanding of the artistic nature that almost everyone can relate to in some way. Though you may not be a trained or professional artist, you almost certainly have an inner Artist with some or all the characteristics that fuel the greats: an appreciation of beauty, a need to express yourself, and an imagination that is continually reshaping the world you live in. The Artist/Creative archetype endows us with a desire to seek out or create beauty, because beauty lifts our spirits and activates positive feelings we thrive on, like optimism and delight.

Much of the time, we fall under the spell of our inner Artist/Creative without even realizing it. How often, for instance, have you walked into a house or an apartment and said to yourself, "If this were my place, I would paint it such and such color, get different furniture, and get rid of those curtains"? Think of the times you have looked at an article of clothing that on the hanger appeared to have come from a yard sale, but then your artistic imagination took over and you accessorized it with the right jewelry, the perfect wrap, and the right shoes, adding just enough color mixed with a touch of "bling." When you let your inner artist explore the hidden potential of the dress, it orchestrated a complete transformation in seconds, turning something undistinguished into a lovely outfit. Or perhaps you experience your inner Artist/Creative in professional settings, imagining how you might execute a creative project. If you have the Artist/Creative archetype, you cannot help reshaping whatever environment you walk into, if only in your mind's eye. Your inner Artist is the source of that impulse to continually enter the wonderland of your imagination and the vast domain of the extraordinary and seek ways to imbue ordinary life with the magic you see through your inner lens.

Ultimately the journey of the Artist/Creative archetype is one of self-exploration—exploring the depths of your creativity and its profound power to transform everything in your life. Whether you are a professional artist or someone who experiences this archetype in a more subtle form, your capacity to create beauty and express your singular voice has no limitations unless you impose them. Your personal journey may find its artistic expression in how you wear your hair or how you design your home or how you wrap presents for your friends, taking the extra time to make bows look like works of art. If you pause for a moment and think of what you do that is unique and special, you will realize that *why* it is unique and special is precisely because you have found a way to turn your particular vision into an art form.

Unique Challenge

Regardless of the Artist/Creative's chosen medium, all individuals who share this archetype are united in needing to confront the fear of not finding an original form of expression, of not having a distinctive vision or voice. When the qualities that make great art are discussed, at the top of the list is originality. The desire to be unique is not reserved for the Artist. It is something we can all relate to because it is a basic human need. The need to find your own voice is a way of asking "What is my unique purpose in this lifetime, the purpose for which I alone was born?" For the Artist/Creative archetype, the quest for originality goes beyond desire: it is a passion, a craving, and for those who are artists by profession, the driving force. Originality becomes the marker by which the Artist defines not only her work but also her identity and value as a person.

This is not to say that everyone with the Artist/Creative archetype has a need or desire to become a professional artist. Has the desire to create original art been a driving force in your life since childhood? Or is it being original as a *person* that is important to you? Some people—you may be one of them—are *living* works of art. Perhaps you dress with a flair, or style your hair with bold color and design, or organize your desk with a sense of artistry. In other words, you create art as you go along. People like you rarely see yourselves as living works of art, but you are. Others may look at how you dress, for example, and think, *I could never get away with that, but it looks great on her,* or *I wish I had her sense of style.*

The Artist/Creative sees art where others may not. I remember spotting a photographer at a historic site. He was carrying only one camera, so there was nothing to suggest he was a professional photographer. But I knew instantly that he was not only a professional but also an Artist. Anyone familiar with the Artist/Creative archetype could see the force of that archetype shining through his choice of subject. I simply *had* to know what he found so interesting in the crumbling castle ruins surrounding us. He told me he had spotted some stones that were the remains of a secret staircase once used by medieval kings and that he was waiting for the light to illuminate them so he could shoot a photograph that would evoke their mysterious origins. Only an Artist could look at a pile of stones and visualize the perfect photograph to communicate 1,300 years of history.

That said, I think the mystery of originality is overstated at times. *Everyone,* not just the Artist, has the capacity to envision the original in his or her own life. But how do you recognize your unique form of expression? And once you identify it, what then?

Among the things I've noticed in working with people through the years is that a majority of them never really take the time to discover what is unique about themselves. People invest enormous energy in exploring their feelings but seldom put that same time and energy into exploring their potential talents. Rather, they often decide in an instant that they have no talent—or at least none worth developing—and that's the end of the discussion. Discovering your original form of expression requires a bit more effort, however.

You can begin by simply observing how you live your life. Think about what you do that you take the time to do especially well. Perhaps you entertain beautifully or make clever birthday cards or decorate your home with style. Instead of discounting your talent in these areas, recognize that you are an artist in them. The Artist/Creative has the potential to develop any talent to the next level, as long as you are willing to invest the time and energy required.

Universal Lesson

The lesson for members of the Creative family is to never disparage or dismiss your talent but to develop your unique artistic gifts. In our society, art is generally regarded as a risky, if not altogether reckless, occupational choice, and any activity that isn't financially rewarding is automatically classed as a hobby. As a result, many Hobby Artists discount their talent simply because they haven't sold a piece of work or performed publicly. Afraid of exposing their creations to the competitive and critical eye of the public, they tell themselves that they need more training, or tragically, they shelve their talent entirely. Then, in order to live with their decision, they tell themselves that they aren't really all that talented anyway. Or they promise themselves they will get back to their artwork "someday" when they have more time.

I have known too many people who have gone down the path of choosing to diminish their talent rather than risk exposing it to others' judgment. We find it difficult to realize that talent is something we do, rather than something we have. Talent is active, in other words—potential energy that lies dormant within us, just waiting to find a path of expression. But because we view talent through the lens of financial viability and consider it without value if we can't make money from it, in many people, the Artist barely has the opportunity to surface, much less develop a truly unique form of expression.

If you are hesitant about showing yourself as an Artist/Creative, remember that all Artists are on a path of uncovering, expressing, and evolving their unique vision. The natural habitat of the Artist/Creative archetype is the imagination itself, and those who lack an artistic eye stand in awe of the Artist's creativity and ability to beautify and transform our world.

But let's imagine that I am speaking directly to *you* for a moment. The Artist in you may not want to enroll in an art class or take up body painting. So ask yourself, "Where is the Artist in me? How do I express the part of me that is artistic by nature?"

I have a very dear friend, a woman I've known for decades. She is the quintessential Artist archetype, not because she paints or draws but because she does everything with taste and flair and would not know how to do it any other way. She's a prime example of making art out of the everyday. I recall being at her home one evening and watching as she effortlessly prepared dinner and set the table. It was a simple dinner, nothing special—pasta and salad. But my enchanting friend's imagination does not have a gear for "ordinary." As she set the table, she arranged candles of various sizes in a charming pattern down the middle. Then she went out in the yard and snipped a few evergreen branches with pinecones to arrange around the candles. When she returned to the kitchen to check on the pasta, I watched as an idea popped into her head. She opened a drawer and scooped up a handful of glitter, then went back into the dining room and sprinkled it on the evergreen branches—not too much, not too little. I marveled at her touch that knew how not to overdo the subtle. Then she called the family to dinner, and while her husband and kids gathered around the table, she dimmed the lights, lit the candles, and turned on some soft background music. Once again, seemingly without thinking about it, she had accomplished perfection.

Artistry takes on infinite forms. Even how we love and nurture others can be done so exquisitely that it, too, becomes an expression of art. The ordinary in life becomes art the moment we use our imagination to see its potential. That is the ultimate talent of the Artist/Creative archetype.

Defining Grace: Creativity

Creativity is the capacity to see the potential in an idea, in a landscape, in the use of color, in the angle of light, in a turn of phrase. It is the defining grace of the Artist. Though many people are surprised when creativity is mentioned as a grace, or spiritual gift, it is in fact a profound one. Creativity has the power to generate art, drama, literature, music, dance, and countless other forms of expression that inspire and transform us.

But how, exactly, do you as an Artist/Creative experience the grace of creativity? You may not be accustomed to thinking about grace in your life, much less creativity as a manifestation of it. But understanding something about the nature of creativity can help you better resonate with its power. For one thing, creativity thrives in a positive environment, an optimistic approach to life. Although we all have bad days and, at times, difficulties that may last for weeks or months, leaving room in your heart for optimism and hope keeps your creative fires burning.

Creativity also thrives in the present. It begins to evaporate the minute we turn to the past for inspiration. It is almost impossible to imagine something new when you are stuck in yesterday's way of doing things.

Inner Shadow

One of the more curious human traits is our disdain for the idea of being ordinary. We will do anything to avoid being thought of as unexceptional or average. Advertisers, in fact, count on this flaw in our nature. Combine a disdain for being ordinary with a passion for originality, and you have the ingredients of the Artist's shadow. If you are burdened with the fear of being ordinary, not only will you find it difficult to birth your inner Artist but should the world not recognize you as special, you are likely to experience primal resentment, often resulting in depression. Perhaps the following story will explain what I mean.

In one of my workshops years ago, I met a man who suffered from chronic depression. I noticed that he was always sketching or doodling, so I asked if he was in an artistic profession. Immediately he grew very defensive and said with a huff that as soon as he had an original idea, he would see it somewhere else. His inner narrative was that someone else was always one creative step ahead of him, so he reasoned that any effort to compete using his artistic talent would be a waste of time. Yet apparently he had mastered one art form—the art of the critic—as he deftly shredded the accomplishments of every artist whose name came up in our conversation. It was impossible for this man to compliment any artists, not because their work was lacking but because they had managed to accomplish what he could not bring himself to do—take the risk to become extraordinary. They had unleashed their creativity and given it full rein to inspire the work that poured out of them. What's more, they were willing to endure the revelation that not everyone in the world was going to love their work. They were daring to live who they really were, no matter what type of public acknowledgment came—or did not come. The man in my workshop, on the other hand, had chosen to repress his creativity out of fear of being viewed as "just another run-of-the-mill artist," as he put it. The irony is that he really hadn't stopped seeking acknowledgment for his talent as an artist—only now he was expressing his artistic talent in a backhanded way, as a harsh art critic.

But how can you quell the fear of being ordinary so that it doesn't prevent you from doing your art? One way is to imagine that creativity is a stream flowing through you, providing you with energy that must be directed into something. If you choose *not* to use your creativity, you are in effect building a dam inside you that prevents the flow of your natural creative insight.

As we have already seen, archetypes are imperatives, demanding that we give them expression. The Artist/Creative archetype calls you to express your creativity in some way. You cannot wait for someone else to acknowledge the Artist in you in order to recognize your own gifts. It is up to you to bring your gifts to the world, no matter how small or large your world. Your talent may end up being recognized by millions of people or only ten, but whichever it is doesn't matter. What matters is that you acknowledged your creative gifts. For the Artist/Creative that is the source of true self-esteem.

Male Counterpart

The inherent impulse for creativity is not gender specific, and the Artist/Creative archetype finds equal expression in men and women. Any differences are generally a product of social convention. If you are a woman in the visual arts, for example, you are more likely to associate success with popular acclaim, whereas a male artist is more likely to view success in terms of money and power. Not that women artists are uninterested in influence or financial success, or male artists in audience approval. But men still find it easier to compete in the arts than women do, and male artists as a rule make more money.

The history of art, particularly the visual arts, is largely a history of accomplished men—Leonardo da Vinci, Michelangelo, Raphael, Rembrandt, and Picasso, to name a few. The reason is cultural: until the 20th century, women were generally not welcome in ateliers and art schools, and unless they had an influential patron, they had to make it on their own. Only a handful of women in the visual arts— Georgia O'Keeffe, for one—have achieved anything like the prominence of their male counterparts. Where women artists have been more successful is in literature and the performing arts. Some of the highest-paid film stars today are women.

Myths of the Artist/Creative

So many myths attach to the Artist/Creative archetype that it is small wonder would-be Creatives are reluctant to even listen to their inner Artist. One stereotype that has been around for centuries is the Starving Artist—the painter or dancer or writer or musician who sacrifices all for art, living a hand-to-mouth existence in a garret somewhere. Think of Vincent van Gogh or Toulouse-Lautrec, Mozart or Edgar Allan Poe, or any of the principals in the classic tale of artistic life, the opera *La Bohème*.

In my work, I have seen evidence of how the Starving Artist myth can stifle the Artist/Creative. I have watched people as they reached a crossroads where they were called to examine how they wanted to spend the rest of their lives. This is an archetypal moment that presents us with an opportunity to lead a more authentic life, based on who we really are and what we have yet to contribute to the world. Those who meet the Artist/Creative at this crossroads often are seized with a sense of urgency mixed with excitement. They can feel their inner Artist/Creative clamoring for attention, begging for release of its creative potential. They long to let the Artist/Creative rip through the confines of their ordinary life and recharge it with untapped power. Yet I have seen these same people turn back or look away, asking themselves, "But how will I support myself? What if this is a foolish dream? What if I lose everything?" The Starving Artist myth can tunnel down into the psyche with dark fears and negativity, convincing us we need a guarantee of success from Destiny itself before our inner Artist/Creative will even try.

A companion to the Starving Artist myth is the myth of the Bohemian Artist—free-spirited, spontaneous, eccentric, and in every way outside the norm. This myth contains a grain of truth in that making art is an introspective process often involving long, solitary hours in a studio or home office. Although many Artist/Creatives are by nature solitary and a surprising number of Performers are very shy offstage, others are as sociable as any other archetype. And if Artist/Creatives like to hang out together, it is because, like most of us, they gravitate toward people who share their interests. Artist/Creatives enjoy the stimulation of exchanging ideas and techniques with other creative people who understand the particular joys, challenges, and responsibilities of leading an imagination-driven life.

While the association between art and poverty has been the view for centuries, today another myth of the Artist is rising alongside it—the Artist Star. Whereas at one time, it was an artist's death that brought fame and fortune, now there are artists and performers earning millions from their work while still very much alive. Think of painters like Julian Schnabel and Damien Hirst, the scriptwriter Aaron Sorkin, pop artists like Justin Bieber and Lady Gaga, and just about any Hollywood star. Far from *la vie bohème*, these artists lead glamorous, red-carpet lives.

Of course, most artists, even professional ones, are not living in the stratosphere alongside the Artist Star. A more down-to-earth portrait of today's working Artist/Creative might show a painter dropping her kids off at school before settling down at her easel, a writer e-mailing his novel to his publisher from his cube at his dot-com job, or a girl band recording a demo in the lead singer's suburban garage.

Yet another myth of the Artist/Creative that refuses to die is that of the Drunken Artist. History is full of creative people whose lives or careers were interrupted or cut short by addiction. Ernest Hemingway, Dylan Thomas, Kurt Cobain, John Belushi, Janis Joplin, and Jimi Hendrix spring to mind. But there is no hard evidence that Artist/Creatives are any more susceptible to addiction than any other archetype. In recent years, as 12-step programs for every sort of addiction have sprung up, many Artists have sobered up and gone on to the most productive work of their careers.

Lifestyle Challenge

Let's be honest: nobody likes to fail. But for the Artist/Creative, particularly the Performer, failure can be an especially bitter pill. As many an actor friend has pointed out, you are only as good as your last performance. And if your reviews are bad or the play falls flat, you may find it that much harder to be cast in the next production. For the Performer, life can sometimes seem like a never-ending audition.

But looked at another way, continual reinvention is the nature of art, an inherent part of the artistic process, and a core strength of the Artist/Creative archetype. Artists are always searching for a more precise or profound or aesthetically pleasing way to articulate their message. Making art is trial and error, painting and overpainting until just the right image emerges from the ashes of what didn't work. The challenge for the Artist is to rise above fear of failure—even failure itself—and begin again and again and again.

With that in mind, it might seem that the Hobby Artist has the best of the Artist/Creative world. If you are making art for yourself, you can dabble, play, mess around, experiment, and pick up or drop any medium or method or instrument you want. It hardly matters if you are good at it or not. You can always move on to another art form or genre without having to worry about humiliation of failure. Your Artist/Creative has the run of your imagination with no one else saying "Stop! Don't go there!"

But in reality, every Artist, whether a professional or a dedicated amateur or an artist of life, is always working within boundaries of some sort—those imposed by your chosen medium, if nothing else. However wild and unfettered your flights of imagination might be, when it comes to putting them down on paper or canvas, you are obliged to work within the discipline of your art form. However inspired the message from your soul, you still have to give it form. The two-dimensional canvas, the proscenium stage, the eight-tone scale, or the rhyming couplet becomes your frame.

Even if your form of expression is redoing the bathroom, the pressure is no less real. You are putting your creativity on display. Your challenge is to go ahead and paint the walls purple and stand by your decision, even when your dinner guests cannot stop whispering about what a mistake you made.

There are bound to be errors, miscalculations, and flat-out mistakes on the way to finding your original voice. But among the great gifts of making art is learning persistence. Keep trying, keep experimenting, and eventually you will be rewarded.

So the lifestyle challenge for the Artist/Creative archetype is not to give up in the face of messes, false starts, do-overs, or failure. Just because an outcome falls short of your expectations does not mean that your talent has failed. Talent is always there, energy ever ready to be tapped. The Artist/Creative archetype is not something that only springs alive in certain contexts. Your life is always your art form.

Recognize Your Archetype: Are You an Artist/Creative?

By now, you must have realized that you don't need to star in a Broadway play or have a painting in the Metropolitan Museum to qualify as an Artist/Creative. True, there are some of you who have never wanted to be anything *but* an Artist or a Performer and have already decided to make art your vocation. The Artist/Creative archetype is vividly alive in you, and you consider art your calling. You may even have enjoyed some—or much—acclaim. Others of you may also identify with the Artist/Creative archetype even if you have not yet established yourself professionally. If you truly have this archetype and remain committed to your art, recognition in some form will almost certainly come.

Still others of you may feel drawn to the arts but remain unsure if you can claim the Artist/Creative as your archetype. Ask yourself: Do you yearn to break new ground artistically, to find your original voice and share it with the world? If so, you very likely fit this archetype, although you need time to refine your mode of expression and consider whether you want to create professionally or for your own pleasure.

The reality is that only a handful of people become world-class artists or performers, but many, many more of us can rightly identify ourselves as Artist/Creatives. You may experience your Artist/Creative at a subtle level, as an inner voice that guides you in making aesthetically pleasing choices in your day-to-day life. Whether or not you ever pick up a paintbrush, tie on a pair of pointe shoes, or try your hand at verse, the Artist archetype can profoundly influence and enrich your life, giving you a thirst for beauty and a passion to manifest it in your surroundings. Creativity demands expression. The creative appetite must be satisfied. The real Starving Artist is not the one subsisting on ramen noodles in order to pursue her lifelong dream but rather your own inner Artist if you fail to recognize, honor, and support her.

Perhaps, however, you are already expressing your creative vision in some way—learning the guitar, shooting a photo essay, spending weekends in your garden, not just planting and pruning but planning the exact right balance of variety and color. It is time to acknowledge these "hobbies of the soul" as art. They are as important to you as air. One signpost of the Artist/Creative is that you identify not just with being creative but also with what you create. For the Artist/Creative archetype, finding form for your creativity is vital to your very being.

"Okay, I may be creative," you concede. "But does that mean I'm an Artist?" If you are still not sure the Artist/Creative is your archetype, check out the behavior patterns and characteristics of the Artist on the next page and see if any of them describe you.

- You see beauty everywhere—the curve of your lover's cheek, the nuance of a shade of green, the sparkle of sunlight on the waves. You are drawn to the unusual in art and architecture. You are inspired by color, texture, and shape. If so, the Visual Artist is alive in you.

- You come alive in front of an audience. When you play an instrument, give a speech, tell a joke, dance the tango, you are communicating with whoever is watching. That is your Artist/Performer looking for a stage.

- You listen to music and your heart soars. You glance at your childhood piano with a pang of guilt. Your iPod is surgically planted in your head. You vocalize at every opportunity—working it, harmonizing, noodling around— and you like what you hear. Your inner Artist/Musician is trying to get your ear.

- You dream of seeing your name on the bestseller list. You've been keeping a journal since childhood. You have poems or a play stashed in a drawer. When something noteworthy happens in your life, your first thought is to write it down. No question, your Artist is a writer. Get busy; update your blog.

- You're ready to make art, not read about it or talk about it.

Step into Your Archetype: Tapping into the Power of the Artist/Creative

Once you decide that the Artist/Creative archetype defines you, the next step is finding the right vehicle to express it. If you are already setting up your next art show or booking a hall to premiere your band, congratulations on tapping into the power of your archetype. You can skip this next bit. But if you're still wondering how to move from thinking about making art to actually doing it, try acting as if you are an Artist/Creative for an hour—or a day or a week. Do something artistic and notice if you feel energized. Hang around with Artist/Creatives and drink in the creative inspiration. No matter how your inner Artist/Creative speaks to you, pay attention and be responsive. By all means, start small. Instead of composing a rock opera, try your hand at writing a song. But don't just come up with a few of bars of melody and a line or two of lyrics, and then stop. If you are an Artist, you have a spiritual obligation to gift the world with your talent. Keep going.

"What if I get stuck, hit a creative block?" you might ask. If you do—and all Artist/Creatives do at times—change direction temporarily. If you were painting, read a book or listen to music. Bake a cake. Brush the dog. Phone a friend. Get up and walk around the room, but don't give up. Sometimes the Artist/Creative in you needs a gentle nudge to emerge.

Perhaps you have not yet started to make art, but you feel restless—unsatisfied with your life and wanting something more, though you are not sure what. Odd as it seems, restlessness may be your Artist/Creative knocking on the door. Do you have a talent that is long past due to be developed or refined? What small step could you take toward connecting with your inner Artist? Most working Artists have a list of projects they plan to undertake. What separates them from the wannabe Artist is that they pick something from the list, make a commitment to do it, and then plunge in—period. Try it.

If you're *still* dragging your feet . . . well, all right. Just this once I will come to your rescue. Here are a few more suggestions for priming the creative pump. Artist friends assure me they work.

- **Listen to yourself.** Turn off all media, silence your phone, and for a few minutes, just sit there. Let the internal chatter die down. What you may discover is a kind of creative void. Since nature abhors a vacuum, ideas and inspiration have a way of rushing in. If you have a question on your mind (say, "What is my Artist/Creative called to do?") plug it in when you sit down, then leave it alone. What you are doing is creating space for your intuition to tell you what you're *really* thinking—what you're worrying about, perhaps, or what you wish you were doing. Do not jump up the minute you feel restless. Give your inner eye time to focus. It may take you a few sessions like this before your intuition yields up a pearl, but trust me, it's worth the wait.

- **Consult your creative childhood.** All children are creative. They have not yet been informed of society's rules or told what color they should paint the cow. Think back to when you were young and what you most enjoyed doing. It was probably something creative—painting, drawing, banging on drums or a toy piano, playing dress-up or ballerina. Or just daydreaming. Plenty of artists I know spent their childhood immersed in an imaginary world of imaginary friends, monsters, and other creatures, and then made up or acted out stories about them. I'm not suggesting that you revert to childhood—art is made in the present with ideas and images that live today. But getting a sense of what got your creative juices flowing back then can help you connect with that creative energy in you now.

- **Browse.** Here's a suggestion I can really get behind: Go shopping. Not with the intent to buy (though if something catches your eye, there's no harm in going back for it later on). The intention here is to give that wonderland of your imagination a wealth of stimulating input. A writer told me that when she's feeling dry she goes to an upscale department store and walks the aisles slowly, as if she were grazing. She lets her eye fall on this scarf, that purse, this display, that shopper with the strange hat and bracelets up to her elbows. After an hour or so she goes back to her desk. Invariably, she said, when she sits down again to write, fresh images come to mind, or a sentence or paragraph she was struggling with untangles itself. An artist told me he spends time in the wholesale flower market. He doesn't paint flowers but giant abstract canvases with blocks of oil paint in vivid hues. He draws inspiration from the riot of color in the flower sellers' stalls.

• **Get a creative job.** Many artists and would-be artists, as they become better acquainted with the Artist/Creative archetype, feel a strong pull to introduce more creativity into their professional life. It may not be practical to drop everything and just paint or write or study dance. But you can look for a job or career path that offers opportunities to use your talents. You may have to be creative about your search, looking beyond the obvious places. But even something seemingly mundane, like a support position in a nonprofit, can be very creative if, for example, you're in charge of decorations for the annual fund-raiser or updating the organization's website and setting up a social media interface.

Even when you are clear that the Artist/Creative archetype defines you, success in finding the perfect way to express it is not guaranteed. Habitual thinking and age-old psychological patterns can throw up roadblocks to creativity when we least expect it. Developing the Artist/Creative archetype to the fullest requires knowing what empowers you to move forward and what can hold you back.

Where You Gain Power

- **Consciously perfecting your singular artistic vision,** your original voice.

- **Sharpening your artistic eye** by experimenting with color, texture, and design.

- **Surrounding yourself with creative people** who inspire you.

- **Trusting your creative instincts completely.**

- **Remembering that you were born for artistic expression.**

- **Seeding your imagination** with input from all the arts, not just your chosen medium.

- **Plugging in to the culture** to open your mind to what's new.

- **Feeding all your senses**—taste, touch, sight, hearing, sensing—to stimulate your creativity and enrich your inner life.

- **Cultivating your intuition,** the Artist/Creative's best friend.

- **Maintaining a positive outlook.** Creativity thrives on optimism.

Where You Lose Power (and how to regain it)

- **Comparing yourself to other artists.** Collaborate, don't compete, and learn from your colleagues.

- **Craving public acknowledgment for your talent.** Focus on making art and the rest will follow.

- **Expecting to realize your artistic vision right away.** Cultivate patience.

- **Giving in to mood swings** that can accompany creative pressure. Get up and move: walking, yoga, sports, dancing, and martial arts can even out your mood.

- **Wallowing in regret.** "I coulda been a contender" keeps you stuck in the past. Stay in the present. Art is made here and now.

- **Equating success with financial gain.** If you can feed the family, support your art, and splurge on the odd night out, be happy.

Checklist for the Artist

☐ I take time to create every day, giving my imagination free rein.

☐ I have friends and mentors who support my artistic vision and creative lifestyle.

☐ I surround myself with beautiful things that inspire me.

☐ I have the patience to create without immediate material gain.

☐ I affirm my talent every day, without worrying about what others think.

Final Thoughts

The Artist/Creative archetype has an inborn calling to contribute to life creatively. It is a privilege to possess artistic gifts and talents. Cultivate yours. To deny them is true suffering.

CHAPTER 5

The Athlete

Archetype Family: *Physical*

Other Expressions: *Tomboy, Adventurer, Outdoorswoman, Competitor*

Life Journey: *To experience life through the power and stamina of the physical body*

Unique Challenge: *To respect the strengths and limitations of your body*

Universal Lesson: *To encounter and confront the vulnerability of the human body*

Defining Grace: *Endurance*

Inner Shadow: *Physical strength is sufficient to attain all life goals.*

Male Counterpart: *Athlete, Thrill Seeker*

Myths of the Athlete: *The Iron Man or Woman; the New Survivalist*

Behavior Patterns and Characteristics: *The Athlete . . .*

- *takes great care of her body.*
- *enjoys physically challenging activities.*
- *is super-competitive but always plays fair.*
- *includes massage and body-centered therapies in her fitness routine.*
- *socializes with other Athletes for inspiration and support.*

Lifestyle Challenge: *Who am I other than an Athlete?*

Life Journey

The Life Journey of the Athlete is to discover a sense of personal power and identity through developing the body. Attaining physical mastery is the foundation of the Athlete's self-esteem. Sports are more than just games or exercise for a true Athlete. As one told me, "Racing against competition is putting 'the reason I was born' on the line." Anyone who has watched Athletes compete understands this. This depth of passion is not unique to today's Athlete. It has been the story of the Athlete archetype going back to ancient Greece.

The Olympic Games of ancient Greece gave birth to the Athlete archetype, defining the ideal of the perfect body as well as the rules for competition. The Olympics celebrated the power and beauty of the male body as well as its strength and endurance. Now, thousands of years later, the template for the perfect Athlete and the honor code governing competition remain intact. We have high expectations that world-class athletes will play fair, be drug free, and never accept bribes to throw a game, even though in reality those standards are sometimes breached.

The ancient Greeks not only gave us the image of the perfect body but also a guide for developing it. Through diligence and endurance the Athlete attains the ideal of near-total control of the human form. For the ancient Greeks, achieving such physical perfection was as close as a mortal could come to being a god. We remain in awe of these toned physiques that make the rest of us yearn for an ounce of such dedication. (I'd settle for getting to the gym three times a week.)

Not that there haven't been significant changes in the athletic arena since the earliest Olympic Games. For one thing, whereas this was once a man's world, the female Athlete is now firmly entrenched in the consciousness of this archetype. Women Athletes are highly respected competitors in a number of sports; in fact, at the Summer Olympics of 2012, there were more women than men on the American team. Though professional women Athletes still have a way to go before they are valued as much as men for their commercial earning capacity, women have proven that they're every bit as skilled and determined to win.

Outside the professional sports arena, women with the Athlete archetype have come into their own. Now the definition of *athletics* includes the full spectrum of activities and occupations that require constant attention to fitness. Dance, all forms of exercise, and body-centered practices like yoga and martial arts rightly come under the heading of athletics, given how physically demanding they are and how much discipline they require. In recent years, the emphasis on fitness and the availability of gyms and exercise studios and health clubs has awakened the Athlete archetype in millions of people. Health clubs are bustling 24/7, as we spin, swim, kickbox, weight train, and bend in a hundred different ways in yoga classes, all to satisfy our inner Athlete's appetite for staying in shape.

Athletes are earth people: you're grounded in your body and comfortable with your physical form. You don't need to be running races or pumping iron to enjoy the benefits of this archetype. Most Athletes like to spend time outdoors and in nature, but even more than that, the Life Journey of the Athlete expresses itself through a very physical, tactile lifestyle. Many of you with this archetype enjoy working with your hands, at things like carpentry and refinishing furniture and home remodeling. You're proud of your strength as a measure of your health and vitality.

Small wonder, then, that aging is the natural enemy of the Athlete. This is an archetype that reaches its peak in its youth, while other archetypes have decades of rich maturing ahead of them. Our culture, of course, is obsessed with youth. Books on anti-aging are surefire bestsellers no matter how bogus the contents, and the cosmetics industry rings up sales in the billions on the promise that a dab of this and a bit of that will melt away decades.

Society's disdain for aging has given rise to the Anti-Aging Athlete, a hybrid of the Athlete archetype that is devoted to running a race against time—a race, of course, that it can never win. Our adoration of youthfulness promotes the belief that pushing the body to extremes can accomplish the impossible and defeat aging itself. Such an extreme goal requires that Anti-Aging Athletes adjust their lives to other extreme requirements as well. Extreme nutrition and obsessive attention to vitamins, health drinks, and rigorous workout and fitness programs all have the underlying goal of turning back time.

Taoism teaches us that all things contain their opposite, and where there is one extreme, the other extreme exists as well. The opposite of the Anti-Aging Athlete who is compulsive about the physical body is the Inert Athlete, who dreams of working out, talks about going to the gym, but chooses instead to sit on a couch and zone out in front of the television set—tuned to sports, no doubt. Inert Athletes long to be connected to their physical bodies: they would give anything to wake up one morning overwhelmed with an irresistible urge to get to the gym. But that just doesn't happen. Inert Athletes are detached from their physical bodies, often dangerously so. More than a few also have the Intellectual archetype and live in their heads, under the self-induced spell that one day they really will work out.

These two extremes, the Anti-Aging Athlete and the Inert Athlete, are shadow offspring of the purist Athlete that reflect the shifting values of the times in which we live. Until we cycle through our obsession with youth and get past our aversion to aging, these hybrid archetypes will be an active part of our collective psyche.

Meanwhile, in a society starved for Heroes, we embrace Athletes as hero substitutes, precisely because they have achieved mega-physical goals. Michael Jordan, for example, rose to Hero status not because he went on the classic Hero's journey in search of inner meaning but because of his larger-than-life skill on a basketball court. He inspired kids to dream big and to push themselves a bit harder on their own home courts. Tiger Woods, on the other hand, was well on his way to becoming one of golf's greatest hero-legends until he fell from grace. It wasn't Woods's skill as a golfer that failed him, however, but his failure as an honorable human being. When Athletes fail to live up to our superhuman expectations, we judge them harshly. No one seems to be indifferent to Athletes, especially other archetypes.

Women Athletes, too, are beginning to reach legendary status, serving as inspiration for Recreational Athletes and aspiring young Athletes alike. Tennis stars like the Williams sisters and Maria Sharapova not only bring attention to their sport but also serve as models of strength and fitness for women who want to get in shape. Most of the people flocking to gyms and sports clubs will never make an Olympic team—nor do they aspire to. But the standards of physical fitness now on display in top Athletes of both sexes are helping to raise the fitness level of the Athlete in every archetype, as we begin to see what is physically possible for the body to achieve.

Obviously, the Athlete archetype today is far more complex than in the days of ancient Greece. What remains a constant, however, is that the Athlete in you is a vital part of your life force as well as being an archetype with a dynamic Life Journey. You may never pick up a tennis racket or swing from the parallel bars or break a record in the 200-meter swim. But your Athlete is that drive in you that longs to smell the ocean or walk the hills or hike through the desert or train for a marathon. At the end of the day, the Athlete archetype is at its best when you treat your body as a resilient, stunning, extraordinary living being that is also aging. The Athlete's Journey is to live well, live wisely, age well, and age wisely, with a healthy, fit body supporting a lively mind.

Unique Challenge

If there is one thing a serious Athlete doesn't want to hear, it's "Your body can't take much more of this." I've witnessed people cross the line from workout dedication to self-abuse because they were determined to force their bodies to build more muscle strength or to heal faster than they were capable of. Whether you are a seriously driven Athlete who works out five or more days a week or a three-hours-a-week-if-I'm-lucky sort, you have to know what your body can and cannot do. You may have ambitions that you are physically unable to realize, regardless of how much you train.

As an Athlete, you have a primary responsibility to your body. You need to know your physical needs from head to toe. If your spine is out of alignment, you need to get regular chiropractic adjustments and consider those treatments an essential part of your workout routine. You have to make sure your gym shoes are the right fit. (Sounds so basic, but unless you are regularly receiving new Nikes as part of an endorsement deal, it's easy to put off buying new ones.) And when your body speaks to you through aches and pains, you need to take note and respond. Because your overall fitness is better than most people's, it's easy to brush off the odd twinge as nothing. But a lot of nothings eventually become something—and it may be something big.

Every serious Athlete will confront breakdowns and be forced to strategize the best healing practices for their body. Ignoring pain signals will make healing more difficult. It tells your body that you don't want your intuition to be connected to the internal message center designed to keep you healthy. We've all read about professional Athletes who played with torn ligaments or broken bones and ended up benched for months.

Accidents happen to physically active people as well as lazy slugs. But as an Athlete, you were born with built-in body awareness. You have the advantage of being naturally centered in your body, naturally comfortable in your physical form, naturally aware of the strength and limitations of your body and what throws you off balance. Your challenge is to stay aligned with your natural center—to pay attention when you are off center and do what you need to do to get back to your core power zone. If you are an Athlete, post this reminder where you will see it often: *No one wins a race when she's out of her power zone.*

Universal Lesson

The lesson of this archetype then is to confront the vulnerability of the body and, therefore, the impermanence of life itself—to fully accept the reality of aging and the inevitable decline of strength and stamina. The Athlete archetype reaches its zenith in the early decades of life, unlike archetypes like the Caregiver, the Teacher, and the Mother/Father, which get wiser and more refined as they mature. By the time the physical body hits its fourth decade, aches and pains begin to compete with speed and agility. The reality of life makes itself known with the gradual diminishing of the very qualities the Athlete values most.

Thanks to improved lifestyle habits, however, the "middle-aged crisis point" is shifting upward. But even the best fitness habits cannot stop the clock. Facing our own physical vulnerability is not something we look forward to. But here the Athlete has more advantages than other archetypes precisely because for you, life is all about what's happening in your body/mind. Your inner Athlete is at its best when organizing health routines and mapping out physical programs that maximize body strength and flexibility, as well as the kind of mental fitness that allows you to achieve maximum health. You are "archetypally designed" for tending to any part of your body that needs attention.

Despite that, the societal pressure to stay young is a far greater challenge to today's Athlete than the actual physical process of growing older. In our world the fear of getting older is so rampant that it's almost impossible to avoid. The mental and emotional aspects of aging are even more aggressive than the physical changes, which can be handled well with nutrition, exercise, and good health habits. Emotional health habits are another matter and require a different type of effort to incorporate into one's life. But for the Athlete, as for any archetype, cultivating a balanced mind is as beneficial as a vital physical lifestyle.

Defining Grace: Endurance

Endurance is the grace of the Athlete. The grace of endurance is an exquisite force that provides you with the will to do the impossible and to carry on through the most difficult times. Endurance is that type of grace that emerges when the task before you is a long road ahead or requires a full commitment of heart and soul.

As an Athlete, you need endurance to maintain, heal, and renew your body, because when you come down to it, staying fit is hard work. Your body needs to be dragged out of bed in the morning, hauled to the gym, exercised into a state in which it's both exhausted and exhilarated, and then given a shower to come back to life. Body maintenance is a commitment, and sometimes it takes months before we see results. Endurance keeps you on task. We've all heard stories of people who have lost a limb yet made the decision to find a way to continue playing sports. Fortified with the grace of endurance, such individuals not only manage to run marathons or swim relay races, but become inspirations to countless others in how to overcome defeat. The South African sprinter Oscar Pistorius didn't win any medals at the

2012 Summer Olympic Games but he made history as the first double amputee to compete alongside able-bodied runners in the Olympics.

The grace of endurance has the power to dissolve the inner saboteur that arises in our weaker moments to slip in the kind of suggestions we shouldn't be listening to, such as, "You're too tired to work out today," or "What difference does one day away from your routine make?" A simple prayer said in one breath—*Give me the grace to endure through my own weak nature*—can give you enough determination to stick with your workout routine or physical therapy program.

Here are a few insights to help you recognize the grace of endurance in your life:

- Endurance enters you through thoughts like *Don't give up.*

- Endurance inspires you in your weakest moments by flooding your mind with spiritual values such as what your life means to others and how much love you have yet to offer, thereby giving you the will to continue.

- Endurance often pulsates in your solar plexus, eclipsing vulnerable feelings of fragility that make you want to step off the more arduous path.

- Endurance builds upon itself, showing you that you can endure anything. You are infinitely stronger than you can imagine.

Inner Shadow

I remember with great clarity the first time I heard the story of David and Goliath, the archetypal figures representing brains versus brawn. It was obvious to me that the lesson was that brains are more valuable than brawn without brains. Yet despite the many times that tale has been told and retold we often overlook the wisdom in it and decide to use brawn for one reason: immediate gratification. Even though we know that pushing our weight around or screaming and yelling accomplishes nothing, the release of tension in the moment gives us the illusion we've gained some ground.

Goliath, of course, is the Bully archetype, an aspect of the shadow side of the Athlete. Intimidated by people he sees as more powerful than himself because of their wits, talent, or character, the Bully resorts to physical strength to humiliate anyone less able-bodied than he. (The female Bully tends to target girls who are social threats.) The Bully Athlete follows the creed that destruction of the physical body is sufficient to destroy a person's will to get up again: knock out your opponent and leave him lying on the mat. What the Bully forgets is that what works *for* him also works *against* him, which is why a Bully can be destroyed with one well-placed punch.

The inner shadow of the Bully Athlete is triggered by deep-rooted fears of defeat, humiliation, and domination. Because these fears are so prominent in his psyche, the Bully Athlete becomes a preemptive strike force, acting to take down any potential targets before they attack him. This particular archetype is now very active in our society, especially in our school systems and on the streets.

There's a recent trend in sports toward more violence, and not just in the boxing or wrestling ring, or in the sanctioned brawling on the football field and in the hockey rink. The ultimate Bully Athlete sport is extreme cage fighting, in which two opponents face off in an octagonal cage 30 feet in diameter to engage in gladiator-type combat using mixed martial arts. Competitors endure broken limbs and other injuries for financial rewards. "Ultimate fighting" has eclipsed boxing and wrestling in popularity, awakening the ancient Roman appetite for blood sport. Though fighters are not allowed to battle to the death, the style of competition, combined with the visual drama of caged combatants, has set a new standard for what an Athlete must accomplish— and endure—to be the best. While it is fair to acknowledge the high level of skill in martial arts among cage fighters, this sport represents the shadow of the Athlete archetype. Like the fight-to-the-death contest in the blockbuster book and movie *The Hunger Games*, cage fighting has awakened one of the darkest primal appetites in the human being: the desire to witness the strong defeat the weak.

Weakness makes us nervous, reminding us of our own vulnerability. We loathe being defeated or thinking of ourselves as fragile. By supporting athletes who symbolically do battle for us—that's called being a fan—we have the sense that somehow we're keeping the weak element in ourselves and in society away from our door. The Bully Athlete, in crushing his opponent, allows us to feel momentarily that we have conquered our own vulnerability and emerged on top.

Male Counterpart

While there are women with the Athlete archetype who enjoy high-risk sports and solo challenges, male Athletes are far more likely to push the envelope when it comes to extreme activities like navigating the globe in a hot air balloon, climbing Mount Everest, racing Formula Ones, or dropping from a helicopter to ski off-trail. For the Thrill Seeker, a high-risk, adrenaline-rush sport is a natural way to achieve a peak experience. As one man told me, "The greater the risk, the greater the concentration. You have to be fully present in what you're doing, or you'll slip up. The consequences of distraction can be lethal." That exhilarating sense of feeling totally alive is the payoff for Thrill Seekers, who put themselves into such totally demanding situations that all other concerns of mind and heart are temporarily silenced. Thrill-seeking sports are a shortcut to gaining a blissful state of consciousness, with maximum physical output.

Myths of the Athlete

The Iron Man or Woman represents the new elite Athlete who has resurrected the best of what this archetype represents: pride in giving your personal best to a sports competition. In the Ironman Triathlon, athletes compete in a race that begins with a 2.4-mile swim, followed by a 112-mile bike ride and a 26.2-mile marathon. Though these men and women are definitely in competition with each other, they also speak with great pride about what it means to complete this endurance test for themselves. An Athlete named Marianne Carrero, who was in training for the Ironman Triathlon, told me, "I'm running the race for me. Every time an athlete makes it across the finish line, all the other athletes are waiting for you, screaming, 'You did it. You're an Iron Man!' Once you achieve that status, it can never be taken away from you."

Physical strength and stamina combined with wits and adaptability are the ingredients that make for the latest addition to the Athlete family, the New Survivalist. Made popular by endless reality-TV programs in which athletically fit individuals tackle ever more difficult and outrageous physical challenges, the New Survivalist portrays yet another primal aspect of the Athlete: our instinct to do whatever it takes to stay alive. At present in our society, physical power is the most celebrated type of strength, and the New Survivalist myth is that physical strength alone is sufficient for survival. Indeed, more than sufficient—it is sweaty, sexy, rugged, and wild. But the truth is that sweaty, sexy, rugged, and wild are not enough for survival. The New Survivalist completely overlooks the strong intellect and emotional stamina that are also essential for navigating a successful life.

These two Athlete hybrids exist at opposite ends of an archetypal pole. The New Survivalist uses his strength to destroy his competition, while the Iron Man or Woman, though no less competitive, is also able to celebrate the skills of fellow Athletes.

Lifestyle Challenge

For serious Athletes, the burning question is: *Who am I other than an Athlete?* The training and discipline it takes to be in peak physical condition leaves little time for anything else. The competitive life of most Athletes is short, so for professionals and dedicated amateurs nearing the end of their careers, it's imperative to make serious plans for the next phase of their lives.

Every one of us is more than a single thing. No matter how committed you are to being a superb Athlete, you are more than what your body can achieve. Even if you earn your living at one of the many athletic-related occupations, whether sports pro, personal trainer, massage therapist, or yoga instructor, that is not the whole of who you are.

We all face the lifestyle challenge of expanding beyond the parameters of our archetypal identity. But for the Athlete, the challenge may be especially poignant, as the strength and skills you relied on so completely begin to fade. It's never too soon for an Athlete to consider what comes next. Just ask the world-class Athletes who, while retirement was still a long way off, used their downtime to open a restaurant, buy into a franchise, start a clothing line, or earn a degree.

What "power" identity or identities other than Athlete do you possess? What other talents or skills do you have that enhance your self-esteem as much as life on the slopes or the playing field? Wisdom reminds us not to put all our eggs in one basket, especially the basket from which we derive our personal power. If illness or injury or, inevitably, age prevents you from participating in the athletic lifestyle you've previously enjoyed, what inner resources do you have to draw on?

Recognize Your Archetype:
Are You an Athlete?

This is another archetype that most people don't have to wonder if they have. Athletes are unmistakable. It's not just the trophies lined up on your shelf or the closet full of sports equipment or even your well-developed muscles that scream Athlete. Just as there are with other archetypes, there are distinctive behavior patterns that tell us an Athlete is in the room.

Even if you're sure you're an Athlete, there may be other people close to you who would like to know more about this archetype. They, or you, can review the behavior patterns and characteristics of the Athlete on the opposite page.

BEHAVIOR PATTERNS AND CHARACTERISTICS OF
THE ATHLETE

- You exercise regularly; staying fit is a vital part of your lifestyle.

- You take great care of your body.

- You listen to your body and respond to physical signals like pain.

- You hold nutrition sacred and make sure you eat right.

- You're super-competitive but always play fair.

- You get your kicks from physically challenging activities.

- You were a tomboy as a kid and probably still are.

- Your work involves sports, fitness, or bodywork.

- You spend leisure time outdoors, running, swimming, climbing, or playing sports.

- Your fitness routine includes massage and body-centered therapies.

- You socialize with other athletically minded people for inspiration and support.

- You organize your life around fitness.

Step into Your Archetype:
Tapping into the Power of the Athlete

As an Athlete you pride yourself on being powerful, but you're aware that power is about more than physical strength and athletic skill. There is also a vital mental and emotional component to athletic achievement. A physically fit body is your ground, the solid platform on which to build fitness. A well-developed intellect and emotional balance make you a fully rounded Athlete, capable not only of achieving prowess at physical activities but also of navigating a successful and fulfilling life.

Here are some guidelines and practices for cultivating all aspects of your Athlete archetype:

- **Stay current.** It goes without saying that you probably know all the latest techniques and equipment for your chosen physical activity or sport. But are you up on current thinking about nutrition, exercise, and sports psychology? New research is coming out all the time that updates and sometimes radically changes what we know about caring for the whole Athlete. Select a few reliable websites and check in periodically. Or set your RSS reader to tag feeds from sites that interest you. The American College of Sports Medicine site (www.acsm.org) offers news, research, and an e-newsletter. *Athletic Insight: The Online Journal of Sport Psychology* (www.athleticinsight.com) reports on new research and has helpful links.

- **Be inspired.** Learn from the greatest sports talents, past and present. Read bios or watch documentaries about iconic figures like Jackie Robinson, Muhammad Ali, Jesse Owens, Billie Jean King, and Lou Gehrig, who broke barriers of race, sex, and debilitating illness to become models of endurance against the odds. What skills did they develop to reach the heights? What challenges did they overcome? What can you take from their stories and apply to your own life or athletic career?

- **Pace yourself.** Work with your body, not against it, so you can stay fit and active and in the game longer. If you don't have a trainer, find someone to help you set up a program geared to your age and activity level that takes into account any injuries you have (or had). Don't settle for a cookie-cutter routine. You'd be surprised how many inexperienced trainers assign a 45-year-old a workout that a 20-year-old would find too challenging. Your goal is to keep yourself performing optimally, whatever your age and fitness level.

- **Cross-train.** Remember what fun you had in gym class as a kid? Every week it was a different exercise or sport: monkey bars this week, volleyball the next, somersaults on the gym mats in between. Instead of sticking with the same physical activity day in, day out, mix it up. Think of basketball stars who play golf, football players who shoot hoops. If you usually play alone, join a team at the gym. If you're a team player, go solo and surf or skateboard. There's no pressure to be any good. Do it for the joy of it, and to keep your mind and body sharp by learning something new.

- **Who am I?** If you're so identified with your Athlete self that you come up empty in other parts of your life, it's time to broaden your self-definition. Look at people you admire and see what makes them tick, where they draw their strength. Don't just check out other Athletes; they may be in the same boat as you. Think about talents you have but never use, interests you've not pursued. Apply the skills you've developed as an Athlete—focus, perseverance, the ability to learn—to other worthwhile activities. Make a game of uncovering more of yourself.

The Athlete archetype is power personified. But maybe you could be managing your power more effectively. Here are suggestions for finding power—and for restoring it if you start to lose it.

Where You Gain Power

- **Sticking to a routine.** You do best with discipline, on or off the playing field.

- **Encouraging others.** Supporting your fellow Athletes raises the bar for everyone. Compete without trying to crush opponents.

- **Being an example.** Young people look up to Athletes. Be an ambassador for fitness or your sport.

- **Being a mentor.** Teaching someone else is a good way to sharpen your skills—and a good way to bond with your kids.

- **Expanding your mind.** You're more than a beautiful body. Develop your mind and spirit, and you'll have more to bring to your life.

Where You Lose Power (and how to regain it)

- **Pushing your body** to the point of doing it harm. Take time out to let your body recover.

- **Being an Athlete in mind only.** Don't just promise yourself you'll begin a fitness program "tomorrow." Recruit a buddy to drive you to the gym and run on the treadmill next to yours.

- **Believing that exercise is preventative medicine.** It's necessary but not sufficient for your overall health and well-being. You also need to eat right, get regular checkups, and stop worrying about what you can't change in life.

- **Being a bad sport.** Sore losers ruin the game for everyone. You'll play better when you remember that the best player wins.

Checklist for the Athlete

☐ I celebrate the Athlete in me by walking or bicycling instead of taking the car.

☐ I accept that my body is aging and love it for what it can do today.

☐ I pay attention to what I eat without being fanatical about it.

☐ I nourish my mind and spirit as well as my body, so I can be a happy, well-rounded individual.

☐ I stick with my fitness program, even when I don't feel like doing it.

☐ I am stronger than I imagine; whatever happens, I will endure.

Final Thoughts

For all true Athletes, this is your time to shine. Through your commitment to your own physical well-being and self-care, you are helping to set a new standard of personal health and individual responsibility. In doing so, you are changing the world for the better.

CHAPTER 6

The Caregiver

Archetype Family: *Caring*

Other Expressions: *Nurturer, Mother, Lover, Sister, Teacher, Rescuer*

Life Journey: *To care for others in ways they are unable to care for themselves*

Unique Challenge: *Fear of being thought selfish or unable to care for others*

Universal Lesson: *To learn when to help and when not to*

Defining Grace: *Compassion*

Inner Shadow: *Feeling resentful and uncared for*

Male Counterpart: *The Caregiver is a yin/yang archetype, equally balanced between masculine and feminine heart energy.*

Myths of the Caregiver: *If I don't help others, they'll think I'm selfish. I have to help people or they won't survive.*

Behavior Patterns and Characteristics: *The Caregiver . . .*

- *never turns down anyone who needs help.*
- *serves as the family caregiver.*
- *chooses a caregiving occupation.*
- *sees helping others as a calling.*
- *is a model of compassion and generosity.*

Lifestyle Challenge: *To care enough about yourself to find out who you really are*

Life Journey

The Caregiver archetype embodies the qualities of compassion, generosity, and an inborn tendency to respond to those who need assistance. Though feelings of generosity and compassion are common to us all, these higher human attributes form the core motivational force of the Caregiver. Members of the Caring family—Caregiver, Nurturer, Mother, Rescuer, Teacher—*thrive* on caring for others. Caregivers respond to the world out of a fundamental instinct that asks, "What can I do for this person? Does this person need me in some way? How can I be of service?"

The Life Journey of the Caregiver is to care for others in ways that help them get on with their lives. It is in the Caregiver's nature to respond whenever anyone needs love, attention, or help. Not surprisingly, this is one of the most beloved archetypes because we all need to be cared for. If you identify with this archetype, then you can be sure that you've been targeted to give and receive love and appreciation in this lifetime.

As a heart-centered archetype, the Caregiver perceives others through an ingrained sense of human fellowship. The Caregiver inherently looks for the good in everyone and seeks to resurrect the fallen. Caregivers are born believers in the power of love to move mountains and heal all wounds. It is virtually impossible for the Caregiver to stop caring about others.

Like no other archetype, this one has the ability to sense the needs of other people, whether family, friends, colleagues, or strangers. It would be just like a Caregiver to notice how exhausted you are and drop by later on with dinner. Drop by *with* dinner, not *for* dinner—they won't stay. The Caregiver intuitively knows when you need rest and a home-cooked meal but not necessarily company and conversation. The Caregiver's exquisite sensitivity to others often baffles people without this archetype. If they were to ask the Caregiver, "Why do you give so much when so often you get nothing in return?" the response would most likely be, "I don't know. That's just the way I am."

And how. If you have this archetype you have a seemingly unlimited store of compassion and understanding. You astound others with your ability to find within yourself the resources to give without question and provide a constancy of nurturing that would deplete just about anyone else. Bottomless wells of strength and stamina, Caregivers are born first responders—often among the earliest to show up at disasters, volunteering their time, energy, and resources to assist those whose lives have been turned upside down by floods, tornados, or other natural or manmade crises. Whether the crisis is a skinned knee or a home destroyed by fire, the Caregiver will be there in an instant with Band-Aids, a blanket, and TLC.

Caregivers are natural nurturers. Many of you can be found in the kitchen, making sure that not only are meals tasty and nutritious but also that mealtimes are emotionally nourishing. Feeding others is the ultimate form of caring for many with this archetype. Chances are a Caregiver has a recipe file stuffed with family favorites that her mother and grandmother served before her.

Men as well as women with the Caregiving archetype fall into the role of parenting with ease—provided they become parents at a stage in their lives when they are prepared to give. Though caring for others comes naturally to Caregivers, they still need to mature into the capacity to give without resentment. If forced into the role of caregiving before they have reached that point, they may find themselves in the uncomfortable position of resenting their own nature.

But for the most part, Caregivers give without a second thought. They can't help it. No kindness or consideration is too small. A Caregiver wouldn't think twice about stopping to corral oranges that had fallen from a shopper's grocery bag, or lending a hand to a mom juggling packages and a squirming toddler. People without the Caregiver archetype might notice that someone needed assistance, but they would only offer it if it were convenient for them, or they might hesitate because they felt awkward approaching a stranger.

It's important to note that the capacity to care for others is not unique to the Caregiver, however. As human beings, we have an inherent need to look after each other. Certain archetypes, however, have the potential to bring caring and nurturing to its fullest expression, and the Caregiver is one of them. The Mother, one of the expressions of the Caregiver archetype, is strongly associated with the caring and nurturing of family. It's also important to mention that just because you have the Caregiver archetype, it does not guarantee that you are mature in your skill at nurturing others or that you don't need caretaking yourself.

Further, not all Caregivers are alike. The caring gene or instinct can make its way into any number of archetypes, since caring is a quality of the heart. But we would be most likely to find the caring and nurturing heart in members of the Caring family: the Caregiver, the Mother, the Teacher, the Sister, the Rescuer, and the Companion.

Unique Challenge

Caregivers are haunted by a deep-seated belief that any act of self-care is the height of selfishness. Because you are naturally compelled to reach out to others, you habitually put your own concerns last. You can get so caught up in helping that you ignore your own hunger or exhaustion. Wired to sense the needs of others, you often fail to pick up messages your own body is sending you and disregard twinges and aches that others would recognize as health alerts. One way to spot a Caregiver is by the person trailing along behind her waving a sandwich and pleading, "But you *have* to stop and eat!" Your unique challenge as a Caregiver is learning to trust what your finely tuned intuition is telling you about your own physical and emotional needs.

If you have the Caregiver archetype, no doubt friends have told you, "You have to start taking it easy. You need to do something for yourself." Most Caregivers love the idea of doing something for themselves—taking a yoga class, getting a massage, going on a vacation. But no sooner does someone suggest it than the archetype takes over, and the Caregiver starts marshalling excuses why that's not about to happen.

The fear of being thought selfish or incapable of taking care of others is an ongoing challenge for this archetype. We all know people, mostly women, who have devoted weeks, months, even years to taking care of a parent or an ailing spouse or child. Invariably, they feel guilty about taking any time for themselves. For the dedicated Caregiver, even an evening out with friends can seem like a betrayal, a serious neglect of duty.

Universal Lesson

If you have the Caregiver archetype, you are on a path of learning how to use your innate capacity for caring to benefit everyone in need, yourself included. A key aspect of this is learning discernment: who to care for, who not to care for, and how to care for others without sacrificing yourself. You must also confront the fear that because you give care to others, no one will ever provide care for you.

Because this is a soul lesson that all Caregivers must learn for their inner development, I can almost guarantee that you will find yourself in situations and/or relationships that awaken this lesson. But if you can look at your life and the challenges it brings through the lens of archetypal wisdom, you will come to realize that everyone who tugs at your heartstrings, everyone you feel compelled to help, is in some way serving your learning, just as you are serving theirs.

A wise Caregiver knows when to give, when not to give, and how to give just what is needed, discerning when giving too much would be the worst thing to do for someone. As a Caregiver who gives generously and compassionately with clarity and wisdom, you can become a powerful force for good in the world, whether your sphere of influence is small or vast, local or global, touching a handful of people or humanity at large. But be advised: It takes time and hard-earned experience to learn when to give, when not to, and when to receive. Contained in those words are some of life's most challenging lessons, but believe me, we all have to learn them.

Defining Grace: Compassion

The grace of the Caregiver archetype is compassion. When it touches the life of a Caregiver, compassion changes the way you view people, inspiring you to give someone a second chance or to spontaneously trust a stranger in a way that even you find surprising. Acting out of character is often a sign that we've been touched by grace. Caregivers are undoubtedly familiar with what I call "grace setups"—bolts from the blue that suddenly move you to respond to a situation with compassion and generosity.

Grace serves another powerful function, as a mystical force that can shift us into a more positive and empowered state of mind. The journey of life takes us through endless opportunities, wondrous encounters, and many adventures but also through our share of challenges and obstacles. Often these challenges turn out to be our greatest blessings in disguise, but while we're going through them, we wonder *How will I ever survive this?* A Caregiver may feel isolated and overwhelmed if she alone is responsible for providing the emotional support for her family. But the grace of compassion can lift her out of that state. It may come as a sudden mental shift that allows her to see the humorous side of the situation. Or it can descend as a "holy rage" that gives her the determination not to be defeated, knowing that however difficult the situation is, it will pass, and she will get through it.

The grace of compassion can overtake us in the blink of an eye, when we stumble on a homeless person huddled in a doorway or read or hear about someone's struggles. Grace gives us a few seconds to pause, breathe deeply, and remind ourselves that just for today, all is okay in our own world, and life is a wondrous journey.

Inner Shadow

It might sound as if the Caregiver is a candidate for sainthood, but even the sainted have flaws, and there is a dark side, a shadow, to all that caring. The inner shadow of giving too much is resentment, accompanied by a deep-rooted sense of being unappreciated. Caregivers, who give so much to others, may themselves feel neglected or uncared for, yet they find it difficult to confront negative feelings of any kind. Afraid they won't be loved, Caregivers are reluctant to show any emotional vulnerability. But unacknowledged feelings have a way of oozing out, and a Caregiver who feels neglected but can't admit it may act out her anger indirectly with passive-aggressive behavior.

Here's a typical example of the Caregiver shadow in action: A woman I know was in charge of human resources for a rather large corporation and was dearly loved for her compassionate, nurturing way of working with people. When her company started downsizing, one of her responsibilities was to help workers who were laid off relocate to other departments. But as more and more people were let go she found it impossible to help them all find new positions. Increasingly frustrated with management policies and her own powerlessness in the situation, she started coming to work late. That first passive-aggressive step led to a second: she became increasingly short-tempered and critical of her co-workers, angry that they seemed oblivious to the suffering she was witnessing every day.

Finally, a good friend and co-worker confronted her, pointing out that she was not just having a few bad days but was in a full-blown personal crisis. It took that confrontation for this woman to finally speak openly about her feeling of failure at not being able to help everyone who needed assistance. From an archetypal perspective, she was having a "Caregiver myth crisis": she believed that she was responsible for the entire life of every person who walked into her office, when in reality, she was only responsible for placing them within her company, a job that she was doing especially well. But because she had appointed herself to such an all-powerful role, when a crisis arose, she collapsed under the demands of her extreme caregiving.

A shadow archetype of the Caregiver is the Enabler. Al-Anon, a 12-step program for family and friends of alcoholics and addicts, is filled with Caregiver/Enablers, most of them women, who have taken charge of an addict's or alcoholic's life, allowing him to continue his destructive pattern of using or drinking. This unhealthy dynamic can be found in any situation in which caregiving is taken to an extreme. As the Caregiver/Enabler gradually assumes responsibility for the needy person's life, the needy person becomes increasingly dependent, and the Caregiver/Enabler ends up with a world-class resentment.

A pattern like this was at work in the life of a woman I met in one of my workshops, who was in marital crisis at the time. She had been married almost 30 years to a man she dearly loved. She described him as loyal, hardworking, a good father—and emotionally needy. She, on the other hand, was vibrant, dynamic, outgoing, and adventurous. This sounds like simply a marriage of opposites, but if we look at it through the Caregiver archetype, we can see a deeper meaning.

The woman said her husband needed a great deal of care and attention, and in the early days of their marriage, that had made her feel needed. Her need-to-be-needed Caregiver found the perfect mate in his dependent Eternal Child. All was fine until 18 years into the marriage when the wife developed breast cancer. Now she was the one who needed attention and support. It was her turn to have her meals prepared and the chores attended to. Though her husband no doubt loved her, when her illness demanded all her attention, he unconsciously resented the neglect, as well as having to give emotional support when his life had been all about receiving it.

How fast their relationship might have healed if the couple had told the archetypal truth: if the husband had been able to admit his resentment that the situation demanded he grow up and care about someone other than himself; if he had been able to admit that he didn't want to break out of his Eternal Child archetype because he was afraid that if he wasn't so needy, his wife would no longer take care of him or love him. And if she had been able to admit her hurt and resentment that her husband couldn't support her when she needed it.

Unfortunately, things didn't work out that way, and instead of confronting his feelings, the husband retreated further into his Eternal Child, leaving his wife to heal in what felt to her like an isolation chamber. Drawing on her own Caregiver archetype, she was able to reach out to family and friends, who loved her through her recovery. But having her husband act in such an uncaring way led to a silent bitterness that took up residence in their marriage like an unwanted boarder who had settled into their spare bedroom.

After we talked, the woman came to see that she had two choices: she could continue to repress her resentment or finally discuss her feelings with her husband. I suggested she work with a skilled therapist, because more than simply sharing hurt feelings was involved: she was attempting the formidable task of cracking the archetypal myths that overshadowed her life and her husband's.

We are all influenced, if not controlled and at times even possessed, by our archetypal patterns. None are more potent than those expressed through the shadow. As challenging as it may be to confront these patterns, our life dramas begin to make more sense when understood as the archetypal narratives they are.

Male Counterpart

Although the Caregiver archetype seems to be more prevalent in women, Caregiving is neither inherently female nor male. Men are as able and, quite frankly, as willing to care for others as women are. Many men who become teachers or coaches, or who enter rescuing professions such as firefighting and emergency medicine, have a genuine need to serve and care for others through their career choices.

Myths of the Caregiver

Like all archetypes, the Caregiver has its own set of myths, or narratives through which the deep self communicates its fears, doubts, and hopes to the conscious mind. The signature narrative of the Caregiver archetype is *If I don't help others, they will think I'm selfish, and I'll disappoint them.* This conviction can land Caregivers in situations in which they feel overwhelmed by the needs of others. Being selfish and disappointing others are the Caregiver's biggest concerns—perceived as failures they find untenable in themselves and others. So regardless of how tired they are, Caregivers won't allow themselves to slow down. Like the Energizer Bunny, they keep going and going—giving and giving without pause.

Overgiving is an archetypal hazard of the Caring family. The mere thought of dialing back their giving or shutting it off altogether creates a crisis of the heart and soul for the Caregiver. People who don't have this archetype can't understand why the Caregiver finds the inability to care for someone such a personally shattering experience. If a Caregiver confides to a friend who lacks a heart-centered archetypal compass that she's exhausted by the demands of caring for someone, the friend is likely to say, "What's the big deal? Just tell them you can't take care of them anymore and they need to make other arrangements."

Such a suggestion would horrify the Caregiver. Even if she were to put a replacement in place, walking away from anyone in need is unthinkable to this archetype. Secretly, of course, many would like to walk away—they're only human. But saying no to a request from anyone goes against a Caregiver's nature. The Caregiver archetype wasn't born to care; it was born to care *too much*.

Still, what to others might seem like a negative trait is built into the Caregiver's archetypal DNA. If you have this archetype you know exactly what I mean. There is no way you would go against the essence of who you are.

To a Caregiver, life is a garden that needs tending, if not mending, and you were put on earth to make sure it thrives. Realistically, it is impossible for anyone, no matter how archetypally fit for the job, to take care of everyone she encounters. A Caregiver who has learned discernment and reflective personal choice can use her finely tuned sensitivity to determine who needs help the most, what sort of help they need, and whether in fact she's the right person to give it. The world supplies an endless stream of people in need of care, but that doesn't mean you have to be the one to respond to every request.

Even the most prodigious giver has finite personal resources, and these must be tended with the same level of attention the Caregiver lavishes on others. A Caregiver can easily fall victim to her own inner narrative, embracing myths like *What will happen to this person if I am not here?* or *What will people think of me if I take some time off?* If you have the Caregiver archetype, a far more productive use of your reservoir of compassion would be figuring out where to invest it so that it will be most effective. And that includes investing some friendly concern in yourself.

Believing that people will fall apart if you're not there to take care of them isn't so much a myth as a medieval spell. When the Caregiver myth goes so deep into the unconscious that it becomes a spell, it's very difficult to shake. One Caregiver told me, "I know if I leave for a weekend, my mom will get sick, and it will be my fault." Like a prearranged contract, her mom did get sick when her daughter left town for a few days. It was nothing serious; the mother had come up with just enough psychosomatic drama to keep the Caregiver locked into giving mode, even when she was away on a break. To break free of the spell, the Caregiver needs to be reassured that if she takes off a day or two, or even a week, the world will not fall apart and neither will the people. Human beings are survivors and remarkably resilient. Sometimes the most caring thing we can do is let others discover within themselves the will and the resources to take care of themselves.

Lifestyle Challenge

Archetypes, as we've seen, aren't just clever labels to toss around at parties. Your archetype is a portal to the deepest part of you, your authentic self. For the Caregiver, self-care is a means of empowerment, a direct line to that authentic self.

One woman told me that all her life she had found herself in the position of having to care for everyone around her. Even as a child, she was responsible for her younger siblings while her parents were at work. It seemed to her that she was never going to be able to escape what felt like a burdensome fate. But then she had a revelation. She connected with her Caregiver archetype and realized that caring for others was not her *fate*, but her *destiny*. It was not some onerous task thrust upon her but in fact a spiritual calling—her life purpose. Looking back, she could see that no matter where she lived or what she did, she drew people to her who needed help, because that was who she was in her deepest being. She was born to help others. She also realized that she had some choice in the matter—a choice about *how* to help. Her Caregiver role didn't call for self-sacrifice, didn't require that she neglect herself. Quite the opposite. She had to learn to say "No" and "Not now" and "I could use some care myself." Once she understood this, she no longer felt burdened by the needs of others but blessed in her capacity to assist them. When she grasped the true meaning of her archetypal identity, she experienced a sense of choice in her personal life that was completely new to her.

Your challenge as a Caregiver is to care enough about yourself to find out who you really are—to be willing to look closely and experience the deeper level of your inherent need and desire to care for others. When you connect with your life purpose as a Caregiver, a transformation occurs. You are largely relieved of resentment you've felt because people haven't cared for you with the same dedication as you've cared for them. And you are also relieved of guilt about taking care of yourself. You come to see that in caring for yourself you are not shortchanging others but rather making sure you have the stamina to care for them.

Recognize Your Archetype: Are You a Caregiver?

As you read through this chapter, did you find yourself nodding in recognition at the descriptions of the Caregiver? If you're still not sure if this is your archetype, take a look at the list of behavior patterns and characteristics of the Caregiver on the opposite page to see if you identify with any of them.

BEHAVIOR PATTERNS AND CHARACTERISTICS OF
THE CAREGIVER

- You are naturally compassionate and concerned with the well-being of others, and you feel compelled to act on those feelings.

- Your greatest strength is nurturing others. You can't say no to a request for help.

- You are the one friends and family turn to for emotional support.

- You are drawn to, or already work in, a Caring field, such as nursing, hospice care, psychotherapy, social work, teaching, cooking, or childcare.

- You end up taking care of others, whether you want to or not.

- You were destined to be the family Caregiver. Even in childhood you looked after your siblings.

- You often give more than you receive.

- You find it impossible to walk away from someone under your care, even in your most frustrating moments.

- You often sense what others need even before they ask.

- You naturally bring out the best in others. People tell you what a good listener you are.

- You see helping others as your calling. You put their needs before your own.

- You serve as a model of compassion and generosity at work in the world.

If you relate to many of the behavior patterns of the Caregiver and the descriptions throughout this chapter, then this is most likely your archetype. You may have thought of yourself as a caring person but never had the realization *I am the Caregiver archetype.* How would knowing you are an archetypal Caregiver change your life?

Self-knowledge opens up possibilities. Embracing your archetypal identity may lead you to rethink practical aspects of your life, such as what kind of job or career to pursue, or how to order your priorities. But it also touches you at a deeper level. Your archetype is a blueprint of your soul's purpose, and connecting with it has the power to transform not only your own life but also the lives of others. In embodying the Caregiver archetype, you are serving as a model of compassion and generosity to the wider world.

Caregivers can be very powerful players on the world stage. People with this archetype often thrive in influential positions because of how attuned to others they are and how well they take care of their employees and colleagues and communities. Some of the best Caregivers are parents, of course, but wasn't Mother Teresa also a Caregiver? Her children were the poor of Calcutta, her Sisters of Charity nuns, the volunteers who flocked to her mission by the thousands—indeed all of humanity, for that matter. And she was as powerful as any world leader.

Step into Your Archetype:
Tapping into the Power of the Caregiver

Once you've identified with the Caregiver archetype it's time to begin expressing it in your life. One way you can do this is by being authentic in how you give. If you give out of obligation—there's a person standing in front of you, desperate for help, so how can you refuse?—the result may in fact do more harm than good, not only to the person you're helping but to yourself as well. Being true to your Caregiver archetype means giving from the heart. Before you rush in to help, consciously pause to check with yourself that you are not simply responding out of habit.

Another aspect of authentic helping is to consider whether your assistance is really what will be best for the person in need. Maybe someone else is better qualified to solve this problem or provide the necessary aid.

Learning how to balance your giving is essential for tapping into the power of the Caregiving archetype. A key aspect of that is making a commitment to focus your caregiving skills on yourself. You can choose to give yourself the kind of nurturing you so easily extend to others. At first, this may seem awkward and forced; you're undoing the habits of a lifetime. But you can start small, with simple actions:

- **Retrain your brain to say no when everything in you wants to say yes.** You're not doing this just to be contrary. It's an essential part of establishing emotional boundaries. (Having porous or nonexistent boundaries is one way Caregivers lose vital energy.) Next time your child demands, "Mom, get me a glass of water," you could say, "No, dear. Please get it yourself." And to the boss who repeatedly waits till the end of the day to ask you to stay late, you could say, "Sorry, I can't tonight. I have plans." Even if it means coming in at dawn the next morning, you will have stood up for yourself and reminded him that you, too, have a life outside the office and he needs to respect your time.

  The beauty of practicing saying no is that it teaches you to make decisions rationally, not reflexively. Furthermore, pausing to think before you act allows you to better assess when the right answer actually *would* be yes.

- **Be discerning.** Pausing before you rush to help also lets you think through the consequences of your actions. You can ask yourself if the person needing help will be okay if you don't step in. You'll learn to recognize the difference between being in need and just being needy. You can consider whether you might actually be more helpful by *not* helping. Would it allow the person to grow stronger through working out her own solution? The Caregiver who continually indulges the Eternal Child will be stuck in the shadow side of the Mother archetype. You've heard the saying, *Give a man a fish and he eats for a day; teach him to fish and he eats for a lifetime.* The Caregiver who habitually overgives should consider if there might be a more instructive way to help.

- **Trust that help will be there for you.** Caregivers have difficulty trusting that others will be there for them. Perhaps it's because people weren't there for you in childhood. But could it also be that you've trained others not to care by rebuffing their efforts to help you? Allowing others to care for you may be the hardest lesson of all for the Caregiver, but your well-being depends on it. When you're sad or lonely and want company, when you're sick and need TLC, when you have to do something that scares you and need support, *ask*. Don't wait for people to sense what you need. Most people aren't as intuitive as you. So be up front: "I need this. Please help." Then stick around until help arrives.

- **Be unavailable.** Here's a challenge for the Caregiver: Go out for dinner and leave your iPad and cell phone at home. Allow yourself to be off duty for a few hours. If you will be so racked with guilt that you spoil the evening for yourself and the rest of your party, line up a backup Caregiver in advance and make arrangements with anyone who has you on speed-dial to call or text your substitute instead. Better yet, give your backup your phone.

- **Get a checkup.** Seriously. Everyone else manages to get to the doctor, but the Caregiver has to be carted off on a stretcher before she concedes that she's not the Bionic Woman. Schedule checkups with your internist and regular visits to the dentist. Allow no one else to come between you and keeping those appointments. If, like most Caregivers, you ignore warning signs that you're headed for burnout, ask a friend or family member to alert you—and make a solemn commitment to heed their warning.

- **Adopt.** No, not a child, unless that's your passion. If your lifestyle permits, consider adopting a pet. Pets need us desperately; a poodle or cockatoo can't make dinner for itself or air out its bed. Pets love us unconditionally, even when we park them in their crates for hours. Rescuing a pet from a shelter is right in character for this archetype. And if you lavish love and attention on a pet, you won't be tempted to smother people with too much care. (For the furry and feathered, there's no such thing as overcaring—and fish won't notice one way or the other.)

As with any archetype, a big part of embracing the power of the Caregiver is understanding what empowers you to move forward in your life and what can hold you back.

Where You Gain Power

- **Consciously deciding when and how to care for someone.**

- **Caring for others out of compassion,** never out of guilt or obligation.

- **Taking care of yourself** so that you have the physical, emotional, and spiritual stamina to care for others.

- **Fully owning your destiny to be there for others.**

Where You Lose Power (and how to regain it)

- **Allowing fear of what others might think control your actions**. Focus on doing, not fretting, and remember that you're doing your best.

- **Caring for others as a means of gaining love or other rewards.** If you feel yourself becoming manipulative, step away until your motivation is pure.

- **Refusing help when it's offered to you.** Just say yes. Remember, the Caregiver's challenge is to take care of herself.

Checklist for the Caregiver

☐ I take time to nurture myself.

☐ I'm committed to caring for myself as much as I care for others.

☐ I'm learning to discern when to help and when not to.

☐ I won't harbor resentment toward those I've chosen to help.

☐ I will happily fulfill my destiny to care for others. I'm grateful for the opportunity to serve.

☐ I appreciate what others do for me and accept their caring with grace.

☐ I will ask for help when I need it and accept it when it's offered.

Final Thoughts

The Caregiver is one of the most loved—and loving—of the archetypes. If this is you, realize that your destiny is to care for others. You will naturally draw to you those who need your care. Recognize that just as you are helping them, they are helping you. They are your teachers in life.

CHAPTER 7

The Fashionista

Archetype Family: *Fashion*

Other Expressions:
Tastemaker, Stylist, Goddess, Model, Diva

Life Journey: *To pursue a life that is not about appearance but self-empowerment*

Unique Challenge: *To develop your inner qualities in tandem with expressions of your external beauty*

Universal Lesson: *To discover how painful it is to be judged for the externals rather than for the quality of person you are*

Defining Grace: *Exuberance*

Inner Shadow: *The Ugly Duckling Who Never Becomes the Swan*

Male Counterpart: *The Gentleman*

Myths of the Fashionista:
Clothes make the person. You don't get a second chance to make a first impression. Rags-to-riches: Pygmalion and Cinderella.

Behavior Patterns and Characteristics: *The Fashionista . . .*

- *loves fashion without being a slave to it.*
- *always looks good.*
- *uses fashion to develop authentic self-esteem.*
- *helps non-Fashionistas find their personal style.*

Lifestyle Challenge: *How do I fashion a lifestyle that reflects who I am and empowers me as a person?*

Life Journey

The Fashionista archetype is another hybrid in our gallery of archetypes. This archetype is new on the scene, coming into prominence as a result of the media, fashion and gossip magazines, the popularity of models and designer clothing, and the power of the Internet. Their combined alchemy has produced an interest in fashion unprecedented in Western history.

Descriptions of the Fashionista as a clothes addict or a clothes-horse are not only inappropriate but inadequate, completely ignoring the hidden and complex soul journey inherent in our leading red-carpet archetype. The Fashionista is the poster child for exploring individuality and self-esteem, the foundation of this archetype's Life Journey.

Tracing the evolution of the Fashionista, we come to see that throughout history, our choice of clothing has had more to do with power than with design. Today's Fashionista is merely carrying on a tradition that goes back centuries.

We humans have an archetypal need to wear something that shows the world our relationship to power. Whether the item is a talisman dangling from a belt—common in ancient days and popular again now—or a family crest worn on a ring or today's high-priced designer shoes, human beings cannot face the world without something that telegraphs our place in society and says, "I have power." When archeologists looking into a newly opened pyramid examine a corpse several thousand years old, they are often able to construct a possible life narrative for the person from just a tiny symbol woven into a fragment of homespun clothing. Was this man a servant? A member of the Pharaoh's court? That one tiny symbol still contains enough identity and power nearly three thousand years later to communicate what the wearer's clothing conveyed to the world back then: *I am a member of the royal household.*

So long before clothing was fashion, it was a billboard for power and identity. Power wear in the old days might consist of warrior dress or ceremonial garb or a shamanic robe. Power wear today is just a variation on the ancient theme. For example, leather, especially black leather, communicates more power than cotton, and designers deliberately use it to convey the power of sex and seduction, the potential for naughtiness and the forbidden.

It's questionable whether any designers are conscious of it, but when they sketch their new collections, they are not just creating stylish outfits; they are also giving form to a psychic energy field of power and fantasy. Poised to buy that piece of psychic energy and power is a Fashionista. Quite without realizing it, the designer and the Fashionista together are engaged in a ritual of power reenacted by people everywhere.

Back in the Middle Ages, everything from the adornments you wore around your neck and waist and wrists down to your horse and sword and the standard you carried revealed at a glance your station in life—whether you were rich or poor, nobleman or commoner, knight or soldier, citizen or foreigner, landowner or serf, merchant or tradesman, captain or sailor, guard or criminal, educated or illiterate. Your clothing told your story, your history, revealing even your successes and failures.

With the Renaissance came the birth of glamour. What we wore began to tell a different story. Out with clothing merely for survival and in with fashion and design. The opening of trade routes to the East provided an array of silks and other luxurious fabrics, and women and men of means began to outfit themselves as a means of adornment. Over the next few centuries, the endless balls and socializing among the kings and queens and their courtiers elevated appropriate dress from "if you have any" to the lavish bustled-and-beribboned confections that adorned Louis XIV's court at Versailles. Louis elevated fashion to a code of conduct so elaborate that not following it down to the last buckle or bow was grounds for immediate banishment.

Dress in the aristocratic circles of Europe earned a reputation for style and elegance, but soon fashion as frivolity and fun evolved into fashion as mystery and intrigue with a risqué flair. Clothing went from simply signaling your social status to serving as a conduit through which to communicate more daring messages of sexual innuendo and strategic power. Is this starting to sound familiar?

Think about the messages fashion today communicates, many of them mixed.

Fashion can be either a shield or a stunning wrap, depending on whether the wearer feels insecure or empowered. The Fashionista clearly recognizes clothing as a symbolic language of power, and if this is your archetype, your Life Journey is not a tale of dress per se, but a saga of self-empowerment. Clothing for the Fashionista is a billboard for self-expression. With every new creation the Fashionista wraps herself in, she is saying, "Look at me, world." She walks down the street scanning the faces of others for feedback, wondering if people like how she looks.

If you are a modern-day Fashionista, you were formed out of two opposing forces. One is the feminist movement of the 1960s and 1970s, which gave you an appetite for freedom of expression and appreciation for your body. The other is the rise of the modeling and cosmetics industries and the fashion press, which together imprinted on the psyche of women the notion that they can never be thin enough but they can be too old. Aging became a woman's worst enemy, second only to the specter of gaining weight. As commercials showed 19-year-old models promising 60-year-old women dewy, youthful skin, the shadow message was, "If you look any older than this, you are toast in the world."

A Fashionista, then, is living a contradiction—your inner feminist is encouraging you to discover your power, while another voice undermines you for the slightest imperfection, real or imagined. Fashionistas who are world-class shoppers—and there are many—often swing into shopping mode when they are in touch with their inner feminist and questing for a sense of self-esteem. Shopping for fashion items is almost never about the joys of spending money, it's about role playing—imagining who you hope to become, when you lose weight perhaps, or you dress up to go out for a special dinner.

Fashion shopping is the ultimate self-empowerment fantasy for many women. And that's precisely why, for the Fashionista, developing your self-esteem is essential. For you, beauty and fashion carry projections of your journey of self-empowerment and inner growth to a degree unmatched in any other archetype. A

Fashionista might very well take a comment such as "That's not the best blouse for you" as a crushing personal rejection, whereas the Artist archetype would be more inclined to shrug it off, or even turn the blouse inside out, adding a backhanded retort such as, "Like it now?" The Fashionista is completely identified with her body and sees the human form as a living piece of art. So if this is your archetype, you first and foremost need to become comfortable in your own skin.

It is essential for you to remember that fashion is not just about knowing what's in style this season and which designer has captured the spotlight on the runway. You need self-esteem to wear any fashion well. For all you elegantly mature Fashionistas out there, remember that you get better with age. Fashion power does not require remaking your body with endless diets or plastic surgery. You can wear your inner power with style, whatever your weight, body type, or age.

Unique Challenge

Most people associate the word *fashion* with beautiful models, expensive clothing, and the latest styles. But that is not why the Fashionista loves fashion. Beyond how stunning, clever, or even outrageous you are at outfitting yourself, the heart of a true Fashionista is individuality—truly knowing who you are and creating a fashion statement that reflects your whole being.

This is an archetype that adores being noticed, admired, and copied. You were born with a knack for mixing and matching pieces, for wearing the unusual, for throwing odds and ends together and making them look like high-end design. Someone lacking your skill might appear to have dressed in the dark, whereas you, with a little imagination and more than a little flair, have converted the ordinary into the stunning with just the right scarf and jewelry. The French would say the Fashionista's effortless style has *je ne sais quoi*—an indefinable quality that makes it attractive and distinctive.

Often when women get together, the chatter turns to the latest styles. And when the most stunning or creative outfit is mentioned, someone invariably says, "I wish I could wear something like that." The woman who is not a Fashionista drools in envy of the woman luxuriating in an outfit that is perfectly suited to her—a simpatico union of power and style. Achieving this is not a matter of being able to afford designer clothing but rather of knowing who you are at your core and what type of fashion represents your sense of personal power. That's the formula for creating the perfect fashion statement, no matter what you're wearing. If you don't believe me, try the opposite approach. Put on a very expensive designer outfit that you love but you know is really not "you," and then see how you feel. Every one of us has come home with shopping bags full of clothing that looked great in the store but which we ended up never wearing. Why? Because the outfit made us feel *powerless* the instant we put it on. Maybe the color was not right for us, or the hemline was wrong, or the style made our hips far more noticeable than we like. Standing in front of our own mirror, we finally conclude that we look awkward in the same dress that seemed to fit us so well in the store.

There is no typical Fashionista. Each of you has your own body type, skin tone, hairstyle, and personality, as well as your particular taste in designers. You may be someone who gravitates toward classic design—an Audrey Hepburn or a Gwyneth Paltrow in sophisticated, ladylike clothes. Or you might prefer eclectic dress—a little of this and a little of that, like the Carrie Bradshaw character in *Sex and the City*. Or you may be devoted to "green clothing" made from recycled and organic products—now considered not only fashionable but socially responsible and therefore very desirable. It's a direction that designer Stella McCartney, a lifelong vegan, is moving in.

As a Fashionista, creating your own fashion statement is not just a hobby. It's core to your identity. It's a projection of the way the Fashionista archetype is expressing itself through you. If you truly resonate with this archetype, then how you dress holds symbolic authority for you in a way that is incomprehensible to other archetypes. The Athlete, for example, is completely baffled by the

Fashionista's need to read the latest fashion magazines. But as a Fashionista, you need to dress yourself as a projection of your inner qualities, as well as in what suits your physical form. You are dressing your spirit as well as your body, in other words.

Even for the Fashionista, however, it's easy to be seduced by the sheer variety of designs available in the marketplace today. But is wearing a design just because it's in style a form of self-betrayal for the Fashionista? Granted, you Fashionistas can get away with more fashion crimes than other people, but the rule still applies: *Dress according to your archetype.* Archetypes hold the key to your fashion comfort zone because they are the engines of your imagination.

For the Fashionista, creating your own fashion statement is as much a matter of developing your inner sense of self as determining what styles are the most flattering to you. The only "rule" you need to follow is to stop letting what other people think dictate how you dress, so you can start letting the true Fashionista inside you come out.

Universal Lesson

The great lesson of the Fashionista is to witness—and learn from—how painful it is to be judged for your appearance rather than for the quality of person you are. No one likes the feeling of being judged, especially for what she's wearing. But let's face it: Fashionistas are pros at this, and it's not your best side. All you need to do is give another woman a quick once-over to decide whether or not she's got taste and style and if she's worth getting to know. Few industries are as jealous and competitive and judgmental as those that specialize in putting people on public display. Judging how others look is the shadow side, the underbelly, of the fashion and beauty business.

One of the most revealing and poignantly honest stories I ever heard was from a Fashionista Model who attended a lecture of mine when she was at a spiritual turning point in her life. She was on the "age edge," as she described it, meaning that because her face was her fortune, time was not her friend. She was approaching the ripe old age of 33, which she said was a bit past middle age in her industry. She was now competing with 15-year-olds for jobs, and the pressure was getting to her.

She told me she had turned to a spiritual path for sustenance after a particularly painful incident. A young model had come up to her after having been through makeup and dress and asked, "Do I look okay?" The girl was a nervous wreck, as it was only her first or second shoot, and she wanted a little reassurance from a seasoned model. "All I had to do was tell her that she looked terrific, because she did, but I couldn't do it," this woman told me. "I could not bring myself to hand over that much confidence to her when I was so intimidated by her youth and beauty. So I told her that she looked okay, but I said it in a tone of voice that communicated just the opposite. I deliberately wanted to disempower her, to make her feel awful about herself. It worked. I saw it in her eyes. The moment she walked away from me, I felt a wave of shame that made me want to run after her and tell her that she looked fabulous, but I couldn't do that either. That's when I knew there was something missing in me. I did not have enough substance, enough 'me' inside to even compliment the new kid on the block. For all I had accomplished on the outside, I was an empty shell on the inside."

As I told this lovely and courageous woman, "empty shells" are not capable of the honesty and self-reflection she had obviously discovered in herself. Though she would probably never find that young model again, she made the decision to look within at her burning envy and tackle what was an ongoing source of personal suffering. So long as she felt so insecure, she would see everyone as a potential threat, regardless of how beautiful or successful she was.

Fashionistas love being looked at as much as they fear being judged or humiliated for a "fashion imperfection" such as being told that the style they're wearing is not becoming. No amount of baubles, bangles, and beads can make dark feelings of envy or emotional insecurity or emptiness evaporate. Dark emotions can turn you into someone like that Fashionista Model, projecting your envious, negative feelings onto others.

Let's face it: you can always find people younger and more attractive than you. But are they kinder or more thoughtful? Those are the qualities that matter, and they're the ones that get better with age. You have to be made of stronger inner fabric than the clothing you're wearing, or the slightest glance will cause you to crumble. Just as important is remembering the way all-consuming envy feels, lest you harm another person with it.

All the high-fashion outfits in the world can't compensate for low self-esteem. However, feeling good about who you are fits into any outfit.

Defining Grace: Exuberance

The grace of the Fashionista is exuberance. Exuberance is experienced as a *sensation:* not an emotion but a sensation of unrestrained enthusiasm and overflowing joy at being *you,* in exactly the package you came in. In other words, you experience a wholehearted appreciation for the beauty and loveliness of your life. The gift of this profound grace leaves you with the realization that you really would not change a thing about who you are or your life as it is.

Obviously, this grace is not about fashion per se, but about how you fashion your whole life. The grace of exuberance heightens your appreciation and enthusiasm for realizing your own innate ability to resonate with the elements of life that sparkle. For all the times you may have wished that things were other than they are, the deeper truth is that if given the chance, most hardcore Fashionistas would change very little. Any of us would like to eliminate chronic suffering, serious illness, and burdensome debt, of course. But when it comes to changing the essential you—who you are at the deepest level—most Fashionistas would not take that option. And if you examined the reasons why, the core would be this: Fashionistas have the innate ability to transform the ordinary into the sensational. You are masters at seeing the potential beauty in other people as well as in yourself.

And this is where the grace of exuberance really shines through. When grace enters your psychic field, no matter which grace, it immediately heightens your natural gifts. Exuberance often expresses itself as a sense of how you could enhance the potential of another person—how your gift for seeing beauty could improve someone else's life. Grace often awakens in you the urge to give, and through sharing your talent for transforming the ordinary, you can realize the depth of your own inner beauty and all you have to offer.

So the grace of exuberance is about awakening beauty in others, as well as discovering the depth of your own inner gifts, which increase the beauty of your own life. Exuberance is heightened when you live in the present time. Focusing on the past diminishes your capacity to recognize the constant flow of opportunities and blessings in your life.

The grace of exuberance is also what you need to connect with when you lose touch with the beauty in your life. Grace can reignite the exhilaration of being alive and reawaken you to the realization that there is no one else in the world exactly like you.

Inner Shadow

The vulnerable zone for you as a Fashionista is competing with some artificial standard of beauty. Runway models are not slender, they're starvation skinny. One facial line is considered grounds for Botox, a patch of cellulite for liposuction. You can become obsessed with the impossible and then use fashion to compensate for feeling like an ugly duckling. When you are in the throes of the ugly duckling syndrome, you either can't shop for anything, or you go shopping and buy everything that's wrong for you. The shadow side of the Fashionista is seeing yourself as a failure physically: unattractive, overweight, old before your time—and therefore powerless. You might as well just toss yourself off a bridge.

Some ugly ducklings live in this inner dark space all the time, and it's a hellhole. When you cannot find anything at all to love about yourself or find anything beautiful within yourself, even breathing is an effort. It's as if some negative image was locked into your mind at an early age, perhaps by an envious or interfering mother who said you should look a certain way, or by playmates who ridiculed you for your appearance.

Anorexia and bulimia are two disorders that are products of the ugly duckling syndrome. The ugly duckling, feeling criticized or rejected for not being the perfect swan, seeks to control her body in the only way she knows how. The ugly duckling shadow is relentless; the voice of imperfection has no limits or boundaries. It will whisper in your ear 24/7 if you let it. For the Fashionista who suffers from the ugly duckling syndrome, even in its mildest form, the essence of breaking free of it is to realize that everyone—and you're no exception—has a true Self within that is a beautiful swan.

Male Counterpart

For all you men who consider yourselves the masculine counterpart of the Fashionista—the Gentleman or the "Metro-male"— much of what I have written about the Fashionista applies to you. The core elements of this archetype do not change because of gender. But the male Fashionista differs in his surface expression of it.

The Gentleman is an archetype that has been around for centuries, and today's Gentleman is the inheritor of a rich legacy of knights and lords embodying elegance, tradition, and ritual. The Metro-male, on the other hand, has no history but is a hybrid created by the fashion and cosmetics industries and the media that cover them. A woman expects a Gentleman to open her door and pay for her dinner, to stand when she comes to the table, to help her with her coat and perform those small but oh-so-caring acts that specifically define this refined archetype. But does any woman expect all that from a Metro-male? I don't think so. He's probably too busy checking his hair in the mirror.

The Metro-male, in a nutshell, has discovered himself and his physical potential. He can be credited with the rise of the male beauty industry, a niche that never really existed before the emergence of this hybrid archetype. The importance of achieving the perfectly sculpted body or having a hairstyle—not just a haircut—skyrocketed as Metro-males hit the covers of magazines and captured Hollywood audiences, eclipsing the classic Gentleman. Along with the Athlete archetype, the Metro-male dominates the media's "sexiest men" listings. The Metro-male's much-touted "softer side" is largely superficial—a growing comfort with grooming, including manicures, pedicures, hair coloring, facials, and even makeup. Whereas the Gentleman's goal is to *pursue* beauty by wearing dashing fashion, the Metro-male's goal is to *be* beautiful, to razzle-dazzle in the latest fashions so that he will be the *pursued*. Whereas romance emanates from *within* the Gentleman—think of romantic legends like Cary Grant or Fred Astaire or Sean Connery—romance is an artificial construct *around* the Metro-male, a projection of image and form because the Metro-male lacks romantic libido. The pride and power of the Metro-male are invested in bodybuilding and style over substance. With the rise of the Metro-male, for the first time in centuries, men and women with the Fashionista archetype are competing over which of them is the more beautiful.

However, as archetypes go, the hybrid Metro-male is a flash in the pan. Long after he has come and gone, the archetype of the innately elegant Gentleman—the Leading Man, the Romantic Lead—will remain.

Myths of the Fashionista

The iconic myths of the fashion world are *Clothes make the person* and *You don't get a second chance to make a first impression*, with *Nothing compares to style* as a close runner-up. You can protest "I'm not that interested in fashion" all you want, but I will respond, "That's absolute nonsense." The truth is, everyone is interested in fashion in some way or another—even if you can't remember the last time you bought clothes. We are not all Fashionistas, but I'll admit that I watch the Oscars to see what the celebrities are wearing, as does most of America. I cannot identify any of the designers, but it doesn't matter. I love to people-watch, and so do millions of other viewers who are as intrigued by the lifestyles of Hollywood Fashionistas as I am. Never mind that most of these women on the red carpet were dressed by stylists: they're living the myth that *Clothes make the person*, and we love watching them play that out.

Yet another myth of the Fashionista is the rags-to-riches story. Two of the most famous versions are Pygmalion and Cinderella. In ancient Greek lore, Pygmalion was a sculptor who fell in love with a statue he carved. As we know the tale from George Bernard Shaw's play and the musical *My Fair Lady*, Professor Henry Higgins takes on the challenge of turning the Cockney flower seller Eliza Doolittle into a high-society lady. His success depends upon Eliza learning perfect diction and perfect etiquette: said differently, she must pass the test of a British Fashionista of her day. As we know, she succeeds at playing the upper-class game while remaining true to herself—and winning the love of her Pygmalion in the process.

In the Cinderella tale, a magical spell, a single glass slipper, and a handsome prince activate the transformation of a young girl into a Princess Fashionista. In this version of the archetypal myth, Cinderella enters the enchanting world where "dreams come true." Cinderella wins the love of the Prince and lives happily ever after. The Cinderella story remains an archetypal classic not only because we love a tale of princess-meets-prince but also because we are so intrigued with the idea of transformation. Is it really possible to go from one presentation of ourselves to another just like that? Can makeup and fashion work the magic of a fairy godmother's wand, or does it require hours of study and practice with no guarantee of success at the end?

Today there are reality TV shows built around the transformational power of fashion and makeup. They can't guarantee you a prince (or princess), but they tap into the myth that the transformed woman or man, outfitted as a modern-day Fashionista, has a far better chance in the social marketplace. At the end of the day, what we learn from the Fashionista is that there is clothing and there is fashion. Clothing is practical; fashion is fun. Clothing does not come with myths, stories, and fairy tales, but fashion does. Fashion has the power to transform the ordinary part of you into the extraordinary, at least momentarily. Fashion casts each of us in our own personal myth. How much fun is that!

Lifestyle Challenge

The creative instincts of the Fashionista are not limited to fashion. In fact, no archetype has a rigidly defined boundary of influence. The characteristics of every archetype—or at least many—blend into the full spectrum of your lifestyle. For the Fashionista, that means a love of fashion might extend to a preference for having a stylish living environment and even a fashionable social life. A fashionable lifestyle might mean being seen at all the right restaurants and nightclubs, or vacationing in trendy places like St. Barts or St. Tropez. But *fashionable* is a state of mind, not a description of an outfit. It characterizes a complex of attitude, style, design, etiquette, and self-image that come together as an overarching approach to life.

Make no mistake, a fashionable lifestyle takes effort to put together and maintain. Your challenge as a Fashionista is creating a lifestyle that reflects who you are and empowers you as a person. You need to feel good in your body, your mind, and your clothing. Your lifestyle needs to be your greatest personal design, because confidence is your greatest accessory.

Recognize Your Archetype: Are You a Fashionista?

You may be a hardcore Fashionista, or you may be someone who just loves pretty clothes, or you may be someone who follows fashion for status. The differences are subtle, in some cases undetectable to the casual observer, but they originate in very different views of the relationship between fashion and power. There are plenty of women who enjoy decking themselves out in the latest styles, rushing to be the first to wear the status designers and most talked-about designs. These women are slaves to fashion, indifferent to the price on the hangtag except insofar as it lets everyone know, "I know the latest fashions, and I can afford them. I wouldn't be caught dead in anything without a designer label." For these women, power lies in the ability to project an image of status and wealth, to pass themselves off as the elite. It is an illusion of power, however. Decking yourself in Chanel head to toe makes you little more than a walking billboard.

This kind of fashion victim is very different from the Fashionista. If you are a true Fashionista, you are less concerned with what is hot off the runway than in putting together outfits that show your personal sense of style and convey what you consider to be the real source of power—an unmistakable sense of who you are that emanates from within. Your way of wearing Chanel might be to pair a Chanel jacket with jeans from a new young designer, a $12.95 T-shirt from a big-box retailer, and shoes that look fantastic but may or may not be from the current season or a recognizable label.

As a Fashionista you know how to make yourself look terrific, no matter what the occasion or the pieces you are putting together. You understand the concept of power dressing: that it is not the iconic watch from the status retailer but an accessory or piece of jewelry that is talismanic, that tells a bit of your personal story. It might be worth a million dollars or have no sticker value but its value to you is priceless. It is expressive of your essence—your sense of beauty, your sense of values, your self-esteem.

As a Fashionista you not only know what looks good on you but you work the same magic for others. Your natural enthusiasm and eye for beauty are gifts you are only too happy to share. Dressing well is merely a fraction of your talent: you have made your whole life your personal fashion statement, the ultimate expression of who you are.

Still not sure you fit the Fashionista label? Take a look at the behavior patterns and characteristics of the Fashionista archetype on the next page and see if you identify with any of them.

- You have a knack for looking fabulous, no matter what you put on.

- You wear your clothing, it doesn't wear you.

- You see fashion as a means to develop authentic self-esteem.

- You are a savvy shopper and love to try new styles.

- You invest in pieces that speak to who you are, not who others think you should be.

- You see the beauty in other people and love helping non-Fashionistas find their personal style.

- You never go on fad diets, preferring to exercise and eat right to stay fit.

- Your shopping sprees are reconnaissance missions, searching for clothing that empowers you.

- You enjoy supporting young talent and other creative designers whose fashions you choose to wear.

- You are often admired (and envied) for your personal style.

- You treat fashion as your personal art form, with your body as your canvas.

- You set your own standards of beauty and avoid comparing yourself to others.

Step into Your Archetype:
Tapping into the Power of the Fashionista

Knowing that you are a Fashionista doesn't mean you will always get it right. Even Fashionistas have design mistakes in their closets or elsewhere around the house. But because for you fashion is about more than what looks good on the surface, you're willing to learn. Here are some suggestions for getting in touch with your inner Fashionista:

- **Clean out your closet.** Nothing is more of an energy drain than too much stuff, except too much stuff we never use. For Fashionistas, the closet can be an energy sinkhole, full of clothing we once dearly loved, pieces with sentimental value, and power items that have lost their mojo. You've heard it before: if you haven't worn it in two years, you probably never will. If you can't bear to part with it, store it for a year. At the same time, be discerning in what you toss. A Fashionista's closet is her archive, often containing iconic designs. Save what is beautiful or beautifully made. Odds are, you'll pull it out one day and wear it again. Or even put it on display.

- **Be ruthless.** One absolute "don't" is hanging on to any piece of clothing because you think you'll lose weight and be able to wear it again. When you do lose weight, you and I both know you will celebrate with a new wardrobe. So give all those slim memories to the thrift shop and get busy getting in shape.

- **Call in the experts.** It's hard for a Fashionista to admit there's something about fashion she doesn't know. But there's no shame in asking for help if your style is in transition or you want to be more adventurous in how you dress. Unless your BFF is a Fashionista with an infallible eye, hire a fashion consultant. It's well worth the investment and could save you plenty in the long run. Someone with good taste and a fresh perspective can cull your wardrobe for what doesn't fit with your self-definition. If dressing your spirit is as important to you as dressing your body, be sure to choose someone in tune with your values.

Be clear about your objectives. Do you want to repurpose your existing wardrobe, or add or replace pieces, or send it all to a consignment shop and start anew? Many fashion consultants have relationships with stores or designers that allow you to buy at discount. Just be sure you don't fall into the trap of thinking you have to go with whatever the "experts" say looks good on you. Remember: most salespeople work on commission, and however helpful they are, at the end of the day their goal is to ring up a sale.

- **Find your colors.** Fashion should be fun. One way to enjoy it and build a more flattering wardrobe is to work with a color consultant or take one of those home courses that tell you which colors look best with your skin tone and hair color. (Don't worry: you will be given a range of shades, so you won't be stuck with mustard if you find out you're a "fall type" who looks best in earth tones.) Wearing clothes in flattering hues is very empowering. A designer blouse in the wrong shade will never make you feel as confident as an old favorite in a color that's right for you. Promise.

- **Play dress up.** Nobody said you have to stick with the same style forever. That's the joy of being a Fashionista. Expose yourself to the full spectrum of design. A friend of a friend spends the odd lunch hour on the designer floor of a high-end department store, trying on couture. She couldn't possibly afford those fashions, but she has developed a very refined sense of color, design, and workmanship that translates into stunning outfits she puts together from her own wardrobe. If you are too shy to try on Balmain and Stella McCartney, attend fashion shows and visit costume displays in museums. You can't touch but you can look. For a Fashionista, beauty is in the eye of the beholder.

• **Make someone beautiful.** There is nothing more empowering than being generous with what you know. Play Pygmalion and help a friend with no sense of style put together an outfit for a special occasion. And don't forget to stop by the makeup counter for a makeover that brings out her natural beauty.

• **Shop alone.** Only you know the image you want to project, the sense of self you want the world to see. Never shop with your mother or any friend who starts a sentence with, "You know, you really shouldn't wear . . ."

Whatever your archetype, an important step in expressing it fully is to find out what gives you power, what drains it, and how to regain it.

Where You Gain Power

• **Creating a lifestyle that's your personal fashion statement.**

• **Giving yourself free rein to try out new styles.**

• **Highlighting your best assets.** You know what they are and how to make the most of them.

• **Staying in shape.** Beauty and fitness go together. Punishing diets aren't the answer.

• **Being decisive.** Your instinct for good design is spot-on. Don't second-guess your intuition.

• **Living in the present.** Trips down memory lane keep you from seeing the beauty around you now.

Where You Lose Power (and how to regain it)

- **Relying on emotional shopping jags** to make yourself feel better. It won't work, and you'll never wear the clothes. Shop only when you're feeling good.

- **Seeking others' approval.** The only approval you need is your own. Cultivate it.

- **Comparing yourself to others.** There will always be someone younger and more beautiful behind you. Focus on inner beauty: that's what lasts.

- **Listening to your inner critic.** When that voice starts saying you're too fat, too old, or have no taste, plug your ears.

- **Ignoring your inner power gauge.** You're automatically attracted to what empowers you. Pay attention to the signals.

Checklist for the Fashionista

☐ I consider my life my personal fashion statement.

☐ I dress to feel empowered.

☐ I'm not an ugly duckling. My mantra is "I'm a swan, I'm a swan, I'm a swan."

☐ I concentrate on developing inner beauty, which lasts.

☐ I enjoy helping others uncover their Fashionista.

☐ I love fashion but I'm not a slave to it. I consider it a means of self-discovery as well as self-expression.

☐ I don't take myself or fashion too seriously. Life—and getting dressed—should be fun!

Final Thoughts

For all you stunning Fashionistas, I have just one piece of advice: become your beautiful self and that will last you all your life.

CHAPTER 8

The Intellectual

Archetype Family: *Thinking*

Other Expressions:
Professional, Student

Life Journey: *To pursue knowledge for the sake of knowledge and discover truth in all its expressions*

Unique Challenge: *To remain open to new ideas*

Universal Lesson: *To discern the difference between reason and truth*

Defining Grace: *Wisdom*

Inner Shadow: *Using intellectual skills to play mind games and compromise truth*

Male Counterpart: *Intellectual*

Myths of the Intellectual: *If I'm a good person, nothing bad will happen to me. There must be a logical reason for everything.*

Behavior Patterns and Characteristics: *The Intellectual . . .*

- *learns for the sheer love of learning.*
- *responds to life with the head before the heart.*
- *looks closely and considers all the options before acting.*
- *cultivates wisdom to improve life for herself and others.*

Lifestyle Challenge: *To not overthink*

Life Journey

What makes the Intellectual tick can be summarized in one sentence: *You have a passion for exploring the power and riches of your mind.* The Life Journey of this archetype is pursuing knowledge for the sake of discovering truth in all areas of life. For the innately curious Intellectual, living in the Internet Age is heaven on earth: it gives you access to endless streams of information. Intellectuals thrive in this data-driven world: your logical home is cyberspace. You can spend hours surfing the web, whether you're doing scientific research, shopping online, posting a blog, or firing off e-mails. Keeping on top of everything requires networking, and to you, time online is a necessity, not a hobby.

The true Intellectual differentiates between data, information, and knowledge. Data are simply facts and statistics, the raw material of information, a grab bag that includes trivia and nonsense as well as facts. Information is the basis of most of our communication with one another. Knowledge is quite another thing, and no one knows that better than the Intellectual. Knowledge is an understanding of the full spectrum of what can be grasped by the human mind. If you are an Intellectual, you are motivated by the pursuit of knowledge for its own sake, by a love of learning and a thirst to understand why things are the way they are.

Today, the world is driven by the acquisition of information for influence or financial gain. But knowledge pursued for its own sake is not practical; there may be no payoff. Such knowledge is pure, enhancing our understanding of fundamental principles like the cycle of nature or the behavior of the planets or the healing properties of certain plants. Acquiring knowledge out of a love of truth defines the Life Journey of the Intellectual.

As an Intellectual, you thrive on good conversation and sharing ideas with other lively minds. Communication is vital to you. But the measure of an Intellectual is not how articulate you are or how many facts you've acquired but how well you're able to integrate knowledge and experience into an overarching understanding and appreciation of life. Instead of viewing the world as a planet populated by isolated people and organisms, the Intellectual sees an intricate web of interconnection. Whereas more heart-centered archetypes feel a warm, fuzzy, we-are-all-one connection to humanity and all of earth's creatures, the Intellectual understands interdependence at a molecular level, mentally and intuitively grasping the scientific structure underlying it all.

The intellect is the source of our ability to reason on all levels: logical, ethical, and moral. For members of the Thinking Family, the intellect is an endless resource, an inner library of information and knowledge that weaves reason and logic with intuitive intelligence.

Intuitive and emotional intelligence are two important expressions of intellectual power that are often overlooked in discussions of intelligence. Both rely on refined intuition functioning in harmony with our five senses. Most of us who live in Western countries have followed a traditional educational path in which we acquire a more or less standard body of knowledge. No such system of education exists for emotional or intuitive intelligence, yet many people, especially women, rely on these highly sensitive capacities as much as if not more than on the workings of the rational mind. There's a lot of debate over whether emotional intelligence is an inborn trait or a competence we acquire. But either way, it seems to be a capacity we can develop. We can become more astute at reading others' emotional signals and more sensitive to their needs. As for intuitive intelligence, we all have the basic equipment for it. Everyone has experienced intuition, the ability to know things with other than the rational mind, but you may never have thought of it as part of a highly functioning intelligence system.

Intuitive intelligence is developed as a result of becoming congruent, of making sure that your words and your actions are consistent with what is in your heart. We're not born congruent human beings. We earn integrity one life choice at a time. It takes courage to give your word and then keep your word, even to yourself. You have to identify your values and spiritual beliefs and make certain your daily choices are in alignment with them. But it is precisely through these choices that you build self-esteem.

Self-esteem, in turn, opens you to intuitive intelligence. Your five senses alone are not skilled enough to spot illusions. Neither is the rational mind. But together, they're able to discern truth. When you can engage your intuitive resources and trust them, you're able to avoid falling for gossip or malicious lies.

You can't meditate or diet or exercise your way into this refined level of consciousness. You must become a congruent person through consciously deciding to confront what is incongruent about you, and then choosing to bring that part of you into alignment.

That great library we're calling the intellect is stocked with book learning, life experiences, common sense, and intuitive intelligence. Together, they enable us to make clear decisions. For many Intellectuals, this storehouse of knowledge brings professional success. But as many people with this archetype discover, being a creature of the mind only goes so far in satisfying your curiosity about *living* a meaningful life, not just thinking about one. Pursuing knowledge and exploring the riches of the intellect inevitably bring you to deeper questions like *What are my real values?* and *What should I be doing with the rest of my life?*

Unique Challenge

For someone who loves learning as much as the Intellectual, you would think it would be second nature to be open-minded. But oddly, keeping an open mind to new ideas can be a challenge for this archetype. The Intellectual's mental library, like a great university, is to a great extent a repository of the past, stocked with the accumulated knowledge of humankind. Intellectuals can be know-it-alls. With such a sharp mind, it's easy to think you're better educated, better read, better informed than almost everyone else, so what would you be keeping your mind open for—or *to*? What is it you don't already know? For the Intellectual Professional, industry-specific knowledge and skills are what give you an edge, so there's little incentive to admit that there's information you don't possess.

Fortunately, for those of you who open your minds, the rewards are considerable. Years ago, I asked a man I knew who had built a very successful business what the secret of his success was. It was very simple, he told me: "I hire people who know more than I do about everything I know this business needs."

Common sense, our most useful form of intelligence, tells us that it's impossible for us to know everything, even about ourselves. We need the input of others—their feedback, their ideas, their wisdom. None of us can navigate life alone. Still, an Intellectual may find it challenging at times to recognize the intellectual talents of another person. And intellectual one-upmanship isn't restricted to the professional world. Personal relationships can be destroyed because two very smart people do something that's not so smart, which is to let their egos take charge of their brains. When that happens, they make foolish choices.

Any of us can get locked into certain ways of thinking as a result of our education or knowledge or even the limits of our information. The easiest position to assume is our own, and it's effortless to reinforce our own beliefs. The art of the Intellectual is to remain open-minded and expansive, always willing to consider new ideas.

Universal Lesson

A characteristic of Western society is that we are in love with our reasoning capacity. The quest to find the reason why things happen as they do and why they're the way they are is practically in our DNA. We just have to know *why*. We assume that behind every event, personal or cosmic, there is a perfectly good explanation.

The need for reasons has led us to direct our inner resources toward attempting to create what can never be achieved—a totally rational, controllable life. Intellectuals are determined to get to the bottom of things or to track something back to the source, as if somehow knowing first causes will allow them to control the outcome of events. It's very characteristic of this archetype to try and find a logical explanation for a health crisis—one trigger event or trauma that seeded the problem. *If I can find the reason why this illness happened, I can find the cure* is the way this line of reasoning goes. This is wishful thinking, of course, a kind of pseudo-rationality. In fact, most everything that happens in life is the result of a complex of causes and conditions—many of them unknown or unknowable. Experiencing the limitations of investing so much energy in finding reasons inevitably brings the Intellectual face-to-face with the Universal Lesson of this archetype: discerning the difference between reason and truth.

If you have the Intellectual archetype, you will be challenged by your rational mind because life is *not* rational, logical, and fair. We all experience mind-exploding events that feel unfair. Why? Because the game of life itself does not revolve around any one of us. There are more than six billion players on this earth, and all of them are included in the unfolding of events. You need your intuitive skills to navigate the paradoxes and mysteries that are hidden in every second of life and every corner of your heart and soul. Relationships are certainly not rational, nor are healing, forgiveness, and following your gut when all the rational odds tell you to do otherwise. And yet, if you look back at the crowning moments of your life, you will see clearly that in many situations rational thinking had little to do with what happened and that following your intuition—whether you realized you were doing it or not—resulted in the best outcome. In other words, it led you to truth. To find truth, don't rely so much on logic and learn to listen to your gut.

Defining Grace: Wisdom

Wisdom is the grace of the Intellectual, the sign of a refined intellect and its most elegant expression. The Wise Elder and the Sage are archetypes that have traditionally been the wisdom-carriers for societies or tribes. Sadly, they don't have an official place in our society. Rather than Wise Elders, we have the elderly, a population of aging adults we consider a burden in our youth-loving culture.

Wisdom comes from knowledge of ancient and timeless truths that have become guiding principles, worthy of living by and passing on to the next generation. My father once took me aside as a child and said, "I've noticed something about you that I think you should know. You have a very poor memory, but that's a good thing, because a liar needs a good memory. So you can only tell the truth in your life. Do that and you will have nothing to worry about."

My dad gave me a big hug after that, but I felt so frightened. Not because he had caught me in a lie—I hadn't told a lie. Rather I thought, *How will I get through life with a bad memory?* Wow. As an eight-year-old, I had to figure out how to navigate my life based on recalling *the exact truth* about everything. I made the determination right there to compensate for my flawed memory. I would take notes; I would study extra hard; I would look twice at things; I would listen extra closely. I would do what I had to do so that I would never risk telling a lie. Looking back, I think how wise my dad was to lock in my commitment to truth at such an early age! I discovered that he had said the same thing to both of my brothers when they were young, and we later laughed about our flawed-memory gene pool. But my brothers, with great wisdom, passed on this same advice to their children.

How does the grace of wisdom serve the Intellectual? Wisdom calls you to think twice before doing harm to another person. It is that voice inside you that in the midst of emotional conflict whispers, "Are you sure you want to say that? Because if you do your relationship may change forever." Wisdom inspires you to consider the consequences of your choices—their effect on your life and the lives of others. The Intellectual archetype, knowing the laws of the universe, understands that once a choice is made, there is no way to stop the cycle of consequences that is set into motion.

It is the grace of wisdom that continually reminds you of unfinished business with another person and when you need to forgive. And it is wisdom that reminds you that for this archetype, integrity and honesty are the foundation of a fulfilling life.

Happily, the Intellectual archetype has such a love of truth and respect for wisdom that even without Wise Ones, this grace will not be lost as long as you're in the world. You revere the Sages of the past, but your own life is also among your finest wisdom teachers. You've accumulated a storehouse of wisdom in your life through your own life experiences. The lessons of truth you've acquired are your wisdom jewels. Wisdom is often hidden underneath our greatest hardships, and it is the Intellectual who understands that the search for wisdom is the true path to healing.

Inner Shadow

The intellect is a clever device, if there ever was one. And oh, is it good at mind games. Everyone plays mind games of one sort or another—we all fall into the trap of trying to outwit this person or one-up another. And even if we're not conscious of doing it, we can be very manipulative when we really want something. But when you look at life as a competitive game in which the smartest man or woman wins—the shadow sport of the Intellectual—at what price comes the trophy?

The reasons why people play mind games could fill this book, but they all come down to variations on greed, pride, envy, and vengeance. The shadow of the Intellectual archetype is acting in such a way that you compromise truth. I love the teaching of the Buddha in which he told his followers never to get attached to the illusions of life but to let the "spectacles" pass them by. In the moment, something can look as if we must have it, we must control it, we must be a part of it or else. Or else what? Buddha would say, "Or else what will happen? Will the world come to an end? Will your life cease to be? Will you never see another sun rise for all eternity?"

The lesson for the Intellectual is never to invest so much of yourself in any situation that you are willing to compromise your integrity in order to maintain the illusion. Once that cycle begins, it is nearly impossible to release yourself from it. The Intellectual frees herself from the shadow by knowing who she is at all times and living from her truth. Remember: Every choice you make in life, from what you eat to what you say to how you judge today's events, sets a cycle in motion that remains in motion forever. Of all the mind games you could play in life, the most important is this one: always tell the truth to others and to yourself.

Male Counterpart

The Intellectual archetype is androgynous, found in men and women in equal measure. But certain expressions of the archetype seem to turn up more often in men than in women.

Male Intellectuals tend to favor reasoning skills over emotional intelligence, as many men view emotions as their vulnerable zone. Emotional thinking takes the edge off the capacity to make sharp business decisions—or so that argument goes. As for intuitive abilities, Intellectual men are as naturally wired for intuition as women—intuition is a human capacity, not gender based—although in our culture, there tend to be more women than men in healing-related fields that rely on intuition. However, the male Intellectual's creative instincts in business, science, medicine, and technology, as well as in the arts, are very much rooted in intuitive intelligence.

The sticking point for many Intellectual males is their view of women Intellectuals. Some men see smart women as threats to their business and their manhood. While it may seem surprising that such a heady archetype as the Intellectual could be so involved in sexual politics, remember that politics of any kind involves intellectual game playing to some degree. Ever since women entered the world of work in any number, rightly or wrongly sexual politics have colored the tenor of business. As more women reach the top in male-dominated industries, men with the Intellectual archetype may feel particularly challenged and greet the rise of super-smart women with ambivalence.

An insecure male Intellectual will hide behind facts, opinions, and stubborn judgments, attempting to control his world with a brittle mind that refuses to hear other views. But a confident man with the Intellectual archetype is likely to be open-minded, welcoming the intellectual input of others. The Intellectual male who is confident but not arrogant is capable of just about anything he sets his mind to.

If this is your archetype, you inspire others and have a gift for spotting good talent and encouraging it, regardless of your own success level. You totally grasp the wisdom of the expression *A rising tide lifts all boats*; in helping one person, you know you are helping everyone. Your self-confidence also allows you to move past your intellect and into the deeper content of your interior life. Comfortable with feelings and dreams, you can view the passing parade of life with perspective and a sense of humor.

An Intellectual male who, like his female counterpart, has developed his emotional and intuitive intelligence has all the ingredients of an integrated human positioned to lead in the 21st century. Add vision and courage, and that guy is set to go anywhere he chooses.

Myths of the Intellectual

For the Intellectual archetype, there is one overarching myth: the belief that life should above all be rational. In support of that grand myth there are three variations:

• If I'm a good person, nothing bad will happen to me.

• There's a logical reason for everything.

• I'm entitled to have good things happen to me because I've paid my dues.

We're all familiar with these myths because they live in each of us to varying degrees. We seek a logical reason for why things happen as they do. Deep in our spiritual DNA, we believe in some way that if we're good, bad things won't—or at least shouldn't—happen to us. Such a belief is why we say things like, "I don't deserve to be treated like this," or "She didn't do anything to deserve that type of suffering." Somehow we associate "bad" or painful experiences with punishment—which assumes, of course, that there's someone "up there" in charge of all cosmic punitive acts.

But just how desperately we can rationalize our behavior was brought home to me by a woman in one of my workshops. She recounted how she had spent her youth caring for her parents and had encouraged them, in their later years, to make her the executor of their will and the sole beneficiary. She had a brother, but in her view, she was entitled to her parents' entire estate, as she alone had taken care of them for 15 years. Her brother, however, had other ideas. At the time of the workshop, he was suing her and intended to continue the lawsuit, draining a substantial amount of her inheritance. Despite the lawsuit, she continued to insist that she was entitled to everything and that was that.

The court hearings went on for almost two years at considerable cost to both siblings. In the end, she received 60 percent of the estate and her brother, 40 percent. According to her, he was satisfied, but she felt cheated and unacknowledged by him for her years of devotion to their parents. Entitlement is a ferocious myth to contend with, no matter how it expresses itself in your life. What this woman couldn't grasp was that her brother had his own reasons for feeling equally entitled to his inheritance and that his reasons in a curious way mirrored hers. That is, while her reasons were based on nurturing her parents out of love for them, his sense of entitlement was based on the absence of parental nurturing. Apparently he thought that if he could not get the love he was entitled to as a child, at least he would get the inheritance he was entitled to.

At the end of the day, we all live in our own inner world created by our own archetypes, stories, myths, wounds, sense of entitlement, and curious system of logic, order, and justice. As an Intellectual, you especially prize logic, order, and control, and you readily internalize myths that have a seemingly rational basis. They make you feel safe. They make you feel as if you have some say-so, some control over how the cosmos operates. More than that, myths that elevate the reasonable to truth allow you to believe that you can keep bad things at bay. To the Intellectual, being smart is a kind of armor that's expected to protect you against the slings and arrows that mortals of lesser mental ability suffer.

The intellect is powerful indeed, but trust in the omnipotence of logic is misplaced. Genius is no protection against the quixotic, irrational nature of real life. Every time someone with the Intellectual archetype tells me "I don't understand how this could have happened to me. I did everything right," my response is, "Why *not* you?" To a mind attached to a reason-based view of an orderly universe, that response doesn't compute. Someone locked in this myth simply doesn't grasp that although there is indeed order in the universe, it isn't based on a system of personal justice.

For the orderly Intellectual, who prefers it when life is wrapped up in tidy bundles, dismantling the myth that we can control the tides of life with good behavior requires a substitute myth: the phoenix rising from the ashes. This, too, is an archetypal narrative, one that tells us that even though chaos will inevitably cycle in and out of our lives, we will have the opportunity to rise again from the ashes of ruin.

The wisest move for the Intellectual in you is to go in search of your own truth. Nobody is better at research, after all. Finding your own truth of redemption is the most rational act of all. Here's a truth to get you started: *Know thyself, and you will know the universe.*

Lifestyle Challenge

For the Intellectual the challenge is not to overthink everything. Put simply, you trust too much in what you think you know, or else you think you know everything and everyone else knows nothing. Either way, the result can be disastrous, not just for you but also for your relationships. A well-balanced Intellectual relates to people through the heart as well as the mind.

One challenge for the Intellectual who overthinks is brain freeze when it comes to decision making. For you, facts and information form a kind of safety net. Armed with the right details, you figure you can't possibly make a wrong decision. The problem is, no amount of facts and figures can guarantee any outcome. But flooding your mind with too much information can make you unable to make any decision at all, for fear of making the wrong one.

One of the more significant consequences for Intellectuals is disconnecting from your intuitive abilities. Intellectuals can create rather compact realities for themselves when facts are their only companions. What's important to realize, however, is that intuition does not necessarily disregard factual information. Rather, it utilizes what is known, blending rational data with energetic data—information from gut instincts. The result is a more complete picture of reality than the one the Intellectual sees when facts are her only companions.

To me, the most serious consequence of trusting your mind to navigate your life on its own is that it prevents you from acting spontaneously on those instructions that flood into you from intuition in an all-out effort to get you to redirect your life. All that's required of you is to say yes to the opportunity you're being offered. But the caveat is that you must act immediately, trusting your intuitive instructions—some call it divine guidance—and walking into the unknown. Opportunities like this can be life changing, sending you down what is not just a completely new life path but also a path of transformation that positions you again and again to trust your intuition along with your intellect. From such a life path, your intuitive intelligence takes form.

Recognize Your Archetype: Are You an Intellectual?

Of course you have elements of the Intellectual. You wouldn't be reading this book if you didn't. But is it your dominant archetype?

You may have mistakenly dismissed the possibility that the Intellectual is your archetype because you think that your IQ isn't high enough or that other people seem to know more than you or have fancier vocabularies, more information about current affairs, or a broader understanding of high-minded ideas. Maybe you think that to truly fit this archetype, you have to have done something significant with your intellect, like earning a Ph.D. or becoming an academic or publishing a book or winning the Nobel Prize.

Those are certainly potential accomplishments of the Intellectual, but they're not the defining characteristics by any means. In fact, sometimes the people with the most awards on the wall and initials after their names are arrogant, closed-minded know-it-alls. And some of the people who genuinely qualify as Intellectuals haven't even attended college—never mind Harvard— or won so much as a spelling bee. They are simply profoundly curious, thirsty for knowledge, and in thrall to the greatest teachings of all time, whether from teachers long dead or from the university of life. Ultimately, if you are an Intellectual you are your own best teacher, the one who holds the key to higher learning and the vast riches of the human mind.

If the qualities described in this chapter sound familiar, welcome to the ranks of Intellectuals. If you would like one more test, just to be sure, see if you resonate with the behavior patterns and characteristics of the Intellectual on the opposite page.

BEHAVIOR PATTERNS AND CHARACTERISTICS OF
THE INTELLECTUAL

- You relate to your world through the life of the mind—ideas, concepts, and information gathered from myriad sources.

- You learn for the sake of learning and the love of pure knowledge.

- You spend hours online, letting curiosity lead you.

- You make decisions using a combination of reason, logic, and intuitive intelligence.

- You are on a quest for truth, for a deep understanding of the secrets of the universe and the fundamental laws of how the world works.

- You continually stretch your mind with reading, lectures, and study.

- You regard painful or challenging times as wisdom jewels, treating failure and mistakes as learning opportunities.

- You approach life like a scientist, testing hypotheses and reaching reasoned conclusions.

- You gravitate toward people with active minds and stimulating conversation.

- You lead a carefully considered life. You look closely before you leap.

- You respond to people with your head before your heart.

- You are cultivating wisdom in order to improve your own life and the world.

Step into Your Archetype:
Tapping into the Power of the Intellectual

In all likelihood, if you're an Intellectual you'll have no trouble stepping into your archetype. You are probably already tapping into its power in one way or another. The key is believing in your Intellectual power and trusting the accumulated wisdom of your own life. Even the most painful or challenging times are learning opportunities. Failure can be put to good use as a beacon to light the way to truth.

Just as you need to exercise your body, you need to keep your mind in shape. You need to be alert to opportunities to deepen your wisdom. If you are currently enrolled in a course of formal study, you are already stretching and challenging your mind. But there are other, less formal ways you can develop your intellectual resources to the fullest:

- **Explore Buddhism.** Don't worry, you won't have to give up your religion or any closely held beliefs. Buddhist philosophy can be studied as a remarkable science of the mind, with teachings and practices that help you unmask blocks to awareness and point you toward the realization of deeper truths. It's worth contemplating whether your life goal is mastery of information or knowledge of your true self and how the world works.

- **Stalk the wisdom seekers.** Intellectuals love to learn from the experts. When it comes to wisdom, thousands of years of teachings are available to anyone with Internet access or a library card. Pick a Sage from any era, any branch of learning, and steep yourself in his or her body of work. Sharpen your wits with classical scholars like Plato, Aristotle, and Thomas Aquinas. Follow spiritual Sages—Jesus, Muhammad, Confucius, Buddha—on a quest for meaning, or mystics like Teresa of Ávila and John of the Cross. Explore human foibles and yearning with literary giants like Shakespeare, Keats, T. S. Eliot, and Eugene O'Neill. Plumb the human psyche with Wise Men like Freud and Jung. Read myths: not just the familiar tales of the Greek and Roman gods but creation myths of Native American and other indigenous peoples, for a grounding in the wellsprings of human life.

• **Form or join a salon.** Many of the deep thinkers of the past met in formal or informal gatherings to discuss great ideas or read from one another's work. Often the most famous salons were hosted by women. Barred from the universities, they used salons as their tutorials. Join other Intellectuals online to probe timely issues, or play Gertrude Stein and invite like-minded people to exchange ideas face to face. (Great excuse for a wine-and-cheese party or an afternoon tea.)

• **Read aloud.** Sure you read. You're an Intellectual. Your place is probably bursting with books and your digital reader loaded to the max. But for a change, read aloud to someone and ask someone to read to you. It's not the same as listening to books on tape. More visceral, more intimate, with a familiar voice giving life to the words. Most Intellectuals process information visually. It's an entirely different experience taking it in through the ears. You pay closer attention, for one thing.

• **Get out of your head.** Sounds obvious: too much time in your mind can make you very one-sided. Play or listen to music. Dance. Take a Zumba class. Walk or run around the park. Go canoeing. Eat a gourmet dinner. Have sex. Free up your mind by engaging your body and emotions. It will open up your thinking.

• **Do something shocking.** Step out of character, in other words. Go to an X-rated movie. Take a primal scream workshop. Write a letter with your nondominant hand. Have an astrology reading. Buy a pair of red shoes (symbol of the deep feminine). What you are doing is breaking the spell of rationality, giving your intuitive side an outing. As you become more comfortable with intuitive intelligence and emotional intelligence, you'll be able to approach life with an integrated mind.

The power of the Intellectual archetype lies in the union of reason and intuition. Consider ways you can empower yourself and what you can do to regain power when you lose it.

Where You Gain Power

- **Staying intellectually active** by attending seminars, reading, keeping up on current events.

- **Staying engaged with life,** connecting with interests that ignite your passion for knowledge.

- **Connecting with people** who stimulate your thinking, especially in new directions.

- **Avoiding boredom** by not doing the same old things or thinking the same old thoughts.

- **Avoiding distractions** and keeping your focus on what's most important to you.

- **Feeding your mind with nourishing input.** Lay off the junk TV and sensationalist media and load up on thoughtful commentary. Read articles and blogs that offer genuine insight.

Where You Lose Power (and how to regain it)

- **Dwelling on yourself.** Make time to engage with other people and open your mind to their ideas.

- **Isolating yourself.** Get out of your head and out of the house to avoid depression.

- **Overvaluing your intellectual capabilities.** Hang around the high-IQ set and realize you're just one among many.

- **Comparing your talents and achievements** to other people's kills ambition. Pursue your own goals.

- **Not paying attention to your intuition.** Intuition is the voice of wisdom. Keep quiet and listen.

- **Thinking failure is the end.** To a great scientist, it's just the beginning. You're a phoenix rising from the ashes.

- **Thinking you deserve better.** Life isn't fair, isn't rational. Don't get angry, get busy with a project.

Checklist for the Intellectual

☐ I don't always have to be the smartest person in the room.

☐ I am open to new ideas.

☐ I appreciate the mysteries of life. I don't need a reason for everything.

☐ I trust my intuitive guidance.

☐ I feed my body and soul as well as my mind.

Final Thoughts

Your Intellectual is an expressive archetype, a part of you that needs attention. Remember that opinions aren't truth but simply emotional offerings—statements of how you feel about things. Knowledge comes from discerning thought, from sober reflection on facts, history, and the wisdom of the ages. A true Intellectual knows how to listen and learn from others.

CHAPTER 9

The Queen/ Executive

Archetype Family: *Royal*

Other Expressions: *CEO, Princess*

Life Journey: *To learn how to be responsible for the well-being of others*

Unique Challenge: *To identify the cause or causes in which it is worth investing your power and influence*

Universal Lesson: *To differentiate between authentic power and illusory power*

Defining Grace: *Generosity*

Inner Shadow: *Compromising your integrity to maintain your throne*

Male Counterpart: *The King*

Myth of the Queen/ Executive: *The Queen/ Executive partnering regal femininity with business acumen*

Behavior Patterns and Characteristics: *The Queen . . .*

- *takes charge of situations for maximum results.*
- *commands center stage without even trying.*
- *uses her influence to empower others.*
- *looks her best at all times.*

Lifestyle Challenge: *Sharing power in intimate relationships*

Life Journey

The Queen archetype has existed in one form or another since human beings first organized themselves into hierarchical roles. This is an archetype with an *inherited* destiny: a Queen's title is bestowed upon her—hence, the word *entitled*—and her power is not personal power but power "on loan," granted by the state. Kings and Queens are symbolic carriers of the collective power of the people they rule, and your Life Journey is about learning to be responsible for the well-being of others.

There are two Queens from British history, Elizabeth I and Victoria, who gave form to the Queen archetype as we know it today. Elizabeth I, daughter of King Henry VIII and Anne Boleyn, ruled for over 44 years in the 16th century. She was the embodiment of power, independence, and utter brilliance, a strategist of the highest order and equally beguiling as a woman. Elizabeth carved out the identity of the Queen as an independent force who commands power over men but is never captured by any one man. She was a woman of intense passions, from wild rages to rapturous love. She was selfish and generous, intuitive and paranoid, farsighted and superstitious—all in the extreme. Larger-than-life qualities and emotions are at the core of the Queen archetype today.

Elizabeth's archetypal successor in the modern world is the Queen/Executive. A new archetype, this is a partnering of a noble force, the Queen, with a contemporary concept of power associated with business and finance, the Executive. The woman who no longer believes she has to compromise her femininity in order to achieve her professional goals, the Queen/Executive represents the quintessential partnership of archetypal power.

Queen Victoria, the second historical influence on today's Royal Family, was nearly the exact opposite of Elizabeth I. While Elizabeth never married, Victoria married Prince Albert, whom she adored, and together they had 9 children and 26 grandchildren who ended up populating the royal houses of Europe. Victoria was the longest-ruling queen in history (although the present queen, Elizabeth II, may just break that record). During her reign, the British Empire reached its zenith, as did the attitude of aristocratic entitlement that remains a characteristic of the Queen archetype. Victorian propriety, etiquette, and elegance transferred in a subtle way to today's women who have a strong Queen operating in their psyches. Queens are drawn to elegant clothing, quality jewelry, and fine dining. Moreover, you feel entitled to have these status symbols in your life. Some Queens will make light of their sense of entitlement, but believe me, they're not joking.

The operative word at the heart of the Life Journey of the Queen is *privilege*. However, privilege needs to be understood on more than one level. The ordinary mind views privilege and entitlement as one and the same. We believe that the more power we attain, the more license we have to behave as we wish. The Queen sees herself as above the laws that govern the rest of us.

But associating privilege with personal power has its pitfalls. As a Queen, the challenge for you is to rise above the temptation to use the power bestowed upon you for your personal gain. Your power may be bestowed by corporations, associations, personal businesses, family, or charismatic individuals, but whatever its source, you need to handle it wisely lest other people suffer the consequences of your self-serving choices. It is in your nature to assume authority over others, influencing their lives by virtue of the decisions you make. The wise Queen takes time to reflect on issues that have far-reaching consequences, especially for the people around her.

And so we come to the second and more intriguing understanding of privilege: namely, the privilege of being in a position of power and influence, however grand or humble your kingdom—your arena—might be. You may have worked hard to *earn* your position, as many Queen/Executives have, but forces greater than you helped you achieve it. For the Queen or King or Executive, the Life Journey also involves learning how to manage a position of power and influence while dealing with the archetypal challenges: vanity, a sense of entitlement, narcissism, and the desire to exploit your position for personal gain.

A stereotypic view of the Queen is that she's a demanding, take-charge type who can only give orders, never take them. Those traits, however, are more likely to be found in the Control Freak or the Bully—shadow archetypes of the Queen—than in a true Queen. The

Queen archetype at its most positive is not dictatorial, like the mad Queen of Hearts in *Alice in Wonderland* who orders people around like puppets. The true Queen may be charismatic, with a personality that commands respect, but she recognizes her responsibility to others and is motivated by a desire to enhance the well-being of everyone in her realm. Positions of authority in business, society, philanthropy, and community work are all logical thrones for a Queen. Even the title of Mom qualifies as a privileged position, if you are the holder of power in the home, the one your family looks to for love and advice.

Despite the status and authority that comes with the Queen archetype, it can be a source of conflict for women. For while we associate the Queen with power, it is the Princess we associate with romance and the delights of being swept away by a Knight in Shining Armor. Often the Queen archetype is seen as unapproachable romantically. What commoner would feel safe approaching a Queen for a date? Your Queen can get mighty lonely at the top unless you continually remind yourself that the finest qualities associated with royalty are benevolence, generosity, mercy, and the power to make things happen for people that they themselves are unable to do.

Unique Challenge

The Queen's challenge is to identify a cause that's worthy of her power and influence. Queens need Queendoms. This is a public archetype and not a reclusive one. Queens want to be seen out and about, and want to be more than just another pretty power force. If this is your archetype, no hanging back for you. The Queen wants to exercise her power and make a difference in her realm. Therefore, you need to invest your energy and passion in something that matters. Unlike the Advocate archetype, you are generally not drawn to political causes, which is ironic considering that historically, rulers and politics go hand in hand. But as a modern-day Queen you are more likely to be attracted to new creative ventures, community projects, social causes, and philanthropic interests.

Diplomacy is yet another arena in which the Queen archetype sparkles. Jacqueline Kennedy Onassis was the quintessential Queen/Diplomat as First Lady, as is a real queen, Queen Rania of Jordan. Queen Elizabeth II is perhaps our planet's last great Queen, the embodiment of noble service to crown and country, and diplomacy personified.

In recent decades, Queen/Executives have emerged in the business arena. As such, you are trendsetters. Like most Royals, the women who manage to create corporate empires receive wide notice. Donna Karan, Vera Wang, Martha Stewart, and Oprah Winfrey are among the leading Queen/Executives in today's business world, with the next generation of women like Tory Burch and Ivanka Trump not far behind. Oprah especially embodies the Queen archetype in that she is known for her far-reaching philanthropic work and acts of benevolence and generosity.

But even though the Queen archetype is identified with projects or business ventures executed on a grand scale, that association can be misleading.

If you have this archetype, you were born to put your creative power out in the world, no matter how small your world. Unless you find or create a worthy venture of some sort, you will go to war with yourself or others. A Queen without a realm has no power zone in which to express the psychic energies of the archetype. You end up feeling useless, consumed by the notion that you were born to do or give something to this world.

Those of you with the Queen archetype (along with the rest of the Royal family—King, Knight, and Princess) are contemporary expressions of the grand archetypes that have shaped our relationship to power and ritual for centuries. Though the setting has changed, rest assured that if you symbolically have royal blood, you are attracted to power, an aristocratic lifestyle, and rituals that symbolize authority, such as having a town car (or your own chauffeur) pick you up at the airport, being greeted by name when you arrive at a hotel, and having the best table in the restaurant reserved for you. You can't resist being treated like a Queen.

Universal Lesson

Learning to be in right relationship to power is the universal lesson of the Queen archetype. Our society is obsessed with power in all its permutations: money, status, authority, influence, fame, the power to destroy, the power to save, the power to change others' lives. We fight tooth and nail to accumulate what we believe will be enough power to secure our happiness and well-being. But as the Buddha taught, it's an illusion to think worldly power offers any such guarantees. Forces far greater than us can shift the winds of power hovering over our lives in the blink of an eye.

Confronting the illusion of power is a particularly potent lesson for the Queen/Executive since this is a power-driven archetype. Two Queens or Kings or Executives in one room are destined for a confrontation: Who is the most powerful? Who commands the most attention? Who is the rule maker? Even a pride of lions can only sustain one king—and then only for as long as he can wield absolute power. Inevitably the young male lions will fight for the dominant position, forcing the defeated males to head off and begin prides of their own. The lesson of mastering your own nature—your own power drive, if you will—is woven into the DNA of the Queen archetype. It is up to you as a Queen to come to terms with what qualifies as power for you and what does not. Is your power based upon the recognition you get from others, or does it arise as a function of healthy self-esteem? Power that comes from an external source is illusory and fleeting, while power that emanates from within is authentic and lasting.

History tells us that most Queens and Kings spent the majority of their reign fretting over who had more power, wealth, armies, and influence. The greatest fear of the powerful is to become powerless. As a Queen archetype, you must confront that fear, as once it is running in your psyche, everything around you becomes a potential threat. A Queen can become uncomfortable, if not physically ill, in situations she finds threatening. Princess Diana suffered from bulimia, manifesting her feeling of vulnerability in the power zone of the British monarchy.

If you have the Queen archetype, you are likely to find yourself in one situation after another in which your lesson is to discern authentic from illusory power. If the choices you make leave you feeling drained and disempowered, then you have given away your power to an illusion. But when the choices you make leave you feeling full and empowered—self-contained but not arrogant—you are on the right path. You are learning how to interact with power while not losing yourself to it.

Defining Grace: Generosity

Generosity is the defining grace of the Queen archetype. This grace needs to be understood for the potential it holds to transform your life. One of my books, *Invisible Acts of Power*, is about the power we have to make a difference in people's lives by responding spontaneously—and often invisibly—to their needs. I wrote it because I wanted to explore my hunch that we are born with an intuitive sense of others' needs that develops with increasing acuity as we become more aware.

Generosity begins with an instinctive response to need: the sight of a needy person or a community hit by natural disaster tugs at your heartstrings. Helping people with food or blankets or a comforting word requires little effort and makes you, the helper, feel good. But generosity at the level of a grace is not about making you feel good. Rather, it is about your capacity to be a change agent in someone else's life, to open doors for other people or help in ways they couldn't help themselves. Queens and Kings often have the power to make things happen for other people. This sort of generosity may take the form of providing introductions or opportunities or even positive feedback that, coming from a Queen or King, makes all the difference in the world to the recipient.

If you grasp the true power of the grace of generosity, you will understand that this power is essentially spiritual. The most profound acts of generosity are those that empower others to realize their potential. You don't need to be a wealthy or powerful Queen or King to access this grace. You simply need to have reached a level of self-empowerment that enables you to recognize that empowering others is your finest achievement and not a threat to your own power.

So the grace of generosity awakens in you when you are in the presence of someone only you can help, because of something you can do, say, or provide. This grace can also inspire you to make humanitarian commitments—to take action in behalf of worthy causes. Further, the grace of generosity can be a silent force that acts within your heart to dismantle beliefs that keep you separate from others. In this way, the generous heart becomes the compassionate heart.

Inner Shadow

The shadow side of the Queen archetype is the pull to compromise your integrity in order to hang on to your power. Dealing with the shadow can be a formidable challenge for the Queen or King, because power and authority are so seductive and addictive—as well as so much a part of this archetype's essential nature. Few Queens or Kings relish the idea of losing control of their realms. The inner shadow of this archetype can awaken in you tremendous insecurity about your ability to maintain your throne, not to mention to keep tabs on all the backbiting and power bargaining that goes on behind the throne. Such activities are notorious in any organization in which power is the main currency. That applies to corporations certainly but even to some nonprofits. When there aren't large sums of money to broker—high salaries, huge bonuses, stock options, profit sharing—jockeying for power assumes greater importance.

The shadow challenge for the Queen or King, particularly Executive power brokers, is that inevitably, at some point the power you will be asked to trade is the power of your own character and values. You can sense the presence of a challenge to your integrity by a feeling of insecurity arising in your gut, accompanied by a downward shift in your behavior. It might start with gossiping about co-workers, thereby introducing mistrust into your realm, and escalate to playing power games like *Who's Closest to the Throne?* Behind this behavior, of course, is fear. Your archetypal challenge is to rise above your fear and slay all your inner dragons. Power gained through compromising your integrity is illusory—easily lost and never worth the effort or degradation involved in acquiring it.

Male Counterpart

The King and Queen archetypes share many power tendencies, yet the King differs from the Queen in that he can enter the arena of politics and "wage war" more comfortably than she can. The world expects aggressive behavior from King/Executives and therefore is not surprised to witness these characteristics, but the same behavior from a Queen/Executive elicits a harsher reaction, given that bold leadership is still seen by many to be at odds with femininity.

When it comes to money and power, it remains a man's world for the most part, and Kings know how to wield these forces while wrapping them in dazzling charm—with the emphasis on the dazzling charm. While men with other archetypes have money and power, Kings have something they don't: the power of enchantment. Modern-day Kings can thank the mythic King Arthur for that archetypal magic dust. Were it not for King Arthur and Camelot, women wouldn't still be so psychically attached to the archetypes of the King and the Knight.

But contemporary Kings are not just about enchantment. King/Executives often envision their professional worlds as lands to conquer or acquire. Corporate executives who absorb one company after another are examples of this archetype. Wall Street bankers are also likely to have the King/Executive archetype, as are politicians and individuals in positions of financial or global power. Like the rulers of old, modern-day King/Executives are driven not just by accumulating wealth but also by establishing a network of power and influence over a realm of people.

All Kings like their castles, no doubt about that. How many times have you driven by a grand mansion and remarked, "My word, that looks like a palace!" Chances are, it was a man with a King archetype—or a woman with a strong Queen—who built the house.

Myths of the Queen/Executive

Even though the Queen/Executive is a new archetype on the scene, it represents an ancient myth of noble femininity giving rise to a new pattern of power for contemporary women. The Queen/Executive partners the feminine power of the Queen as a regal force through history with the masculine power symbolic of today's corporate executive. This partnership allows women to attain leadership positions without feeling they must act like men—or dress in power suits—in order to gain a seat in the boardroom.

Because this is such a new archetype, society has yet to create positive myths reflecting the rise of powerful, successful women. Only now are we calling forth women who clearly embody this archetypal duo. Oprah Winfrey and Barbara Walters, for example, are regal, feminine, and known to be kind and generous to the people they work with, while also embodying the skills and savvy of today's business people of either sex. Queen/Executive women are moving into influential positions in finance and politics, as well as the corporate world. There have been isolated examples of women in top political jobs—Israel, India, and the United Kingdom, for example, have all had women prime ministers, and Germany does today. But none of those women has embodied the Queen/Executive archetype as the full expression of feminine power in harmony with political or corporate power. There is a lingering assumption that a woman has to compromise the feminine side of her life—marriage, partnership, and motherhood—to some extent in order to achieve a successful position in the world arena.

Although the Queen/Executive is an archetypal pattern whose time has come, achieving the perfect balance can be a challenge.

It requires you to maintain your femininity while simultaneously drawing on what are considered masculine power qualities like being direct, a tough negotiator, and willing to undertake financial risk.

It takes time and experience for an evolving archetype to work its way into a society. One sign that a new archetype has taken hold is that people begin to create stories or produce films in which the lead character is exactly that archetype. In *The Devil Wears Prada* the Queen/Executive is portrayed as a powerful, ruthless magazine editor based, according to some, on the longtime *Vogue* editor Anna Wintour. We have yet to see a film that portrays a benevolent Queen/Executive.

But that time is coming. As more Queen/Executives grow comfortable in positions of power, they will cease having to fight to stay empowered as executives and women at the same time—and film and television will no doubt reflect that.

Lifestyle Challenge

Power plays destroy as many personal relationships as infidelity. The Queen archetype, more than any other, confronts the lifestyle challenge of when and how to turn her power off. This is no small obstacle. If you are a Queen with a career, you are accustomed to leading and being direct. And being the center of attention. Queens are accustomed to taking up all the oxygen in the room. So for this archetype, it can be very difficult to come home, wind down, and fall into the role of equal partner. (But if you think the alternative—coming home to a bossy Queen—would be pleasant, think again.)

As a Queen, your challenge is to take off your crown and return to being a woman in your personal relationships. By definition, that means being committed to cooperation, compromise, and mutual support, whether with an intimate partner or family members or friends.

Recognize Your Archetype:
Are You a Queen/Executive?

Now that you know that the Queen is an archetype associated with elegance, style, and the grace of generosity, and not some eccentric control freak barking orders at her minions, do you consider yourself a Queen? Perhaps you see yourself more in the Queen/Executive, a savvy businesswoman and leader who embodies strength and femininity in equal measure.

Though no one would ever call the Queen a homebody, people with this archetype love to entertain—"to hold court"—particularly at home, where you can take charge of the event down to the last detail. Bringing people together and caring for the group is inherent in this archetypal pattern. As a Queen, you take your responsibilities seriously, recognizing that ultimately a noble Queen is the servant of her subjects and that your decisions and behavior can have a dramatic effect on the lives of others. Your greatest power and authority come from doing all you can for those who rely on you.

But make no mistake, for all your generosity, if you have the Queen archetype, your true home is center stage. Even if you are simply waiting for a bus—or your limo—you command the attention of those around you. For that reason, you always need to look your best—no running out to the market in sweats and no makeup. Above all, you need to exercise your power with utmost integrity. For better or worse, the Queen is always in the spotlight.

Does this sound like you? If you're still not sure, review the list of behavior patterns and characteristics on the opposite page to see if they seem familiar.

BEHAVIOR PATTERNS AND CHARACTERISTICS OF
THE QUEEN/EXECUTIVE

- You take charge of situations for the sake of achieving maximum results.

- You make things happen for other people. Empowering others is your finest achievement.

- You are direct in dealing with others and let people know what you expect of them.

- You absolutely must look your best at all times.

- You pour your energy into worthwhile causes. You're never just a figurehead.

- You use your influence to make a difference in people's lives.

- You work hard to uphold your character and values.

- You naturally end up in positions of power and authority, even when you don't actively seek them.

- You can be intimidating to people who are trying to get close to you.

- You command center stage without trying, wherever you are.

- You have a demanding job that puts you in the public eye.

- You may not give orders but no question, you're the person in charge.

Step into Your Archetype: Tapping into the Power of the Queen/Executive

The Queen archetype is about power. And your challenge is to discern authentic power from power that is illusory. By nature, you have a sense of entitlement, but you will need to learn to wear your crown—to embody your power—with humility. The Queen who truly understands that power is a privilege, not a tool for dominance over others, is capable of great things in whatever domain she chooses, whether it is public service, philanthropy, the corporate world, her community, or her family.

The divine paradox for an archetype that is so power-driven is that you find your greatest power and authority in doing your best for anyone who would benefit from your ability to empower others. Your Queen is most powerfully expressed when you can make a difference.

Here are some ways you can tap into the power of the Queen and make the most of your archetype:

- **Be a mentor.** Some companies and organizations have formal mentoring programs, but even if yours doesn't, you can undoubtedly find someone who would welcome your support and guidance. Not only will you be giving someone the benefit of your experience but like a true royal you will be passing along the power of your position to the next generation. Every organization has a legacy but sometimes the accumulated wisdom gets lost if there is no formal mechanism to ensure succession. How you mentor isn't the issue—it could be as simple as meeting for coffee or lunch once a month, or as intense as daily tutorials via text and e-mail. The Queen and King are never better than when using their influence and inner resources to develop and empower others. What you have, others want and cannot get anywhere else. Happily, you feel it your duty to share it.

- **Pick a cause, any cause.** It's almost impossible to imagine that with this archetype, you don't already have a favorite cause or enterprise in which you're heavily invested. But if you're between causes, pick something to get involved in without delay. As a Queen you have a formidable amount of creative power, and if it isn't contained in some sort of venture, you're likely to take your frustration out on yourself or anyone who's handy. A Queen needs a Queendom; it's as simple as that. It doesn't matter what you choose for your realm, as long as it has integrity. And your involvement doesn't have to be on a grand scale. It could be answering phones at a crisis center or guiding visitors around a community garden. But the philanthropic drive is so strong in this archetype that I wouldn't be surprised if you're running the organization before long. Your access to resources—and skill in persuading others to invest them in your project—is unmatched.

• **Cook dinner for two.** Okay, order in, if you must. But one way or another, spend a quiet evening at home with your significant other or a dear friend or beloved family member. Turn off your phone, turn down your megawatt personality, and have a few hours together without distractions or—this is important—power plays. (Power plays drain your energy, but serving others fills the well.) Intimacy and give-and-take are not inherent strengths of the Queen, so you need to make an effort to develop these skills. Try not to focus on what you hope to get out of the evening. Just be there, fully present.

• **Redecorate the castle.** You have to sleep somewhere, as well as have a place to host those parties that Queens (and Kings) are renowned for. This archetype is generally meticulous about details, so why not make sure that your dwelling lives up to the regal standards you've set for the rest of your life? Make it truly a place to hold court. I can see it clearly: sumptuous fabrics, arresting artwork, the finest furniture you can afford—elegant and luxurious without being ostentatious. You treat your guests like royalty and send them home thinking that there's no place as magical as your castle. (Short of Buckingham Palace and Versailles, there probably isn't.)

Since power is so important for your archetype, take a tip from wise Queens and Kings and make choices that leave you feeling full and empowered rather than drained. Here are some ways to tap into your power effectively:

Where You Gain Power

- **Cultivating self-esteem,** so you can hold your center when attention comes your way, as it inevitably does.

- **Investing your power and influence in worthwhile endeavors.** A Queen without a Queendom feels useless, which can lead to acting out or depression.

- **Forming intimate relationships that are mutually supportive.** Queen power can be intimidating. Don't blind others with your radiance but create a partnership of equals.

- **Putting your integrity above all else.** Your goal is not to maintain your throne but to use your power and authority to serve others.

- **Exercising humility.** It's an illusion to think you have any more power over others than you do over the winds and tides.

- **Being generous.** Generosity without any thought of benefit to yourself is the grace of the Queen.

Where You Lose Power (and how to regain it)

- **Pursuing the illusion of power.** Money and status are illusory. They could disappear in a flash. Real power comes with enlightened self-awareness.

- **Misusing your power for personal gain.** Other people's needs are a Queen's first priority.

- **Gossiping.** Negative talk is a slippery slope, leading to fear and paranoia. Don't give in to envy and backbiting.

- **Forgetting that power is an aphrodisiac.** Hold your center when confronting the illusion of power.

- **Allowing privilege to give you a false sense of entitlement**. You're an ordinary human being with ordinary human issues, no matter how big your realm.

- **Indulging in power plays.** This is the easiest way to compromise your integrity and that of any group you're representing. Corporations have fallen like soldiers on a battlefield in recent decades because the King/Executives have stolen the treasury for themselves. Keep your hands clean.

Checklist for the Queen/Executive

☐ I take care not to abuse power for personal gain.

☐ I use my influence wisely, to provide opportunities for those who need them.

☐ I value my relationships and am working on being a true partner.

☐ I remind myself that even though I feel like royalty, I'm an ordinary person with ordinary human concerns.

☐ I'm investing my energy where I can make a difference in the world.

Final Thoughts

Remember that what makes you an archetypal Queen is not riches or palaces or commanding a nation but the capacity to make life better for others through your generosity. A true Queen is a positive change agent in her world. You can be as much a Queen at home with your partner as you are in running a business. It isn't the setting that makes you a Queen. You bring your Queen into whatever room or situation you enter. So if you have the Queen archetype, make the most of the Queen in you.

CHAPTER 10

The Rebel

Archetype Family: *Rebel*

Other Expressions: *Maverick, Feminist*

Life Journey: *To break through barriers that restrict the fundamental liberties of the human spirit*

Unique Challenge: *To find your personal voice and form of expression*

Universal Lesson: *To transcend the need to engage in power struggles as a way of expressing authority in your life*

Defining Grace: *Justice*

Inner Shadow: *Confronting an ego motivated by a personal agenda to gain attention*

Male Counterpart: *Rebel*

Myth of the Rebel: *Prometheus*

Behavior Patterns and Characteristics: *The Rebel . . .*

- *speaks out against discrimination and oppression.*
- *challenges injustice.*
- *wears bold and daring styles.*
- *does things in nontraditional ways.*
- *chooses the less-traveled road.*
- *introduces radically new ideas into the culture.*
- *thrives on making waves.*

Lifestyle Challenge: *To not allow the Rebel in you to control your emotional nature.*

Life Journey

The Rebel simply cannot be contained in one definition. This is a complex archetype that has evolved various expressions to keep pace with the ever-changing power dynamics of human society. But regardless of how many expressions there are, the core characteristics of the Rebel remain the same, beginning with something that all human beings share: a rebellious streak.

As humans, our survival instincts awaken early on and are honed and refined by our parents and other elders through basic instructions. We're taught to avoid fire and not play with matches, to lock doors and not talk to strangers, to buckle seat belts, to not put nasty things in our mouths, to wash our hands and brush our teeth. Then, as we mature, we're introduced to the rules of personal responsibility. We learn about right and wrong, good and evil, and the fundamentals of moral reasoning. And then we reach puberty. In our teens, our yearning to break away from the family and become independent is acute. And so, like clockwork, a rebellious streak emerges. Hairstyles and clothing become outrageous. We start experimenting with drugs and alcohol, and become sexually active. Extreme attitudes and behavior are all part of the rebellious years. We are programmed to break out of the restrictive patterns of the elder generation and forge new patterns of our own.

But as we enter adulthood, we have to confront our teenage rebellious streak and take control of its impulsive hair trigger. Many people simply outgrow their teenage rebellion years. But others choose to nurture their rebellious streak, absorbing it into their personality. These individuals go through life controlled by a knee-jerk rebellious attitude, and their behavior can damage their relationships and professional opportunities. They have defined their sense of personal power by the rule *No one is going to tell me what to do*. Every suggestion, no matter how well meaning or useful, is perceived as an effort to control them.

But there are other individuals whose teenage rebellious streak matures into a stronger and less fragmented Rebel archetype. There are four primary expressions of this Rebel: the Noble Rebel, the Anarchist Rebel, the Social/Civil Rebel, and the Feminist Rebel. If you consider yourself a Rebel, you'll relate to one or more of these descriptions in a deeply personal way.

The Noble Rebel

The Noble Rebel is intimately connected to the founding of the United States. For this archetype, rebelling against tyranny, injustice, inhumanity, and social evil is a calling. The Noble Rebel openly challenges the oppressive ways of governments or dictators or other controlling systems in order to secure freedoms for a repressed group or society. Among the Founding Fathers of the United States were lawyers, a philosopher, writers, farmers, entrepreneurs, scholars, a renowned inventor, and a general. For all their differences in background, personality, wealth, and religious belief, what held them together was their bond as Noble Rebels. All of these individuals had the fire of the Noble Rebel burning in their souls, urging them to fight for a cause greater than their own personal interests.

The founding of a nation based upon the rights of the human spirit was the grandest "human experiment" ever to take place on earth. These Noble Rebels were aware that they were attempting to give birth to what could be the most inspiring nation of all time, while simultaneously committing treason against their government. So deeply did they believe in this cause, however, that in signing the Declaration of Independence, they agreed to "mutually pledge to each other our Lives, our Fortunes, and our Sacred Honor." Every one of the signers of the Declaration was willing to lose everything he had—even his life—for the cause he so believed in.

Close to 75 years later, Henry David Thoreau articulated the creed of the Noble Rebel in his immortal essay on civil disobedience, asserting that individuals should not allow governments to overthrow their consciences or make them agents of injustice.

The Nobel Rebel doesn't challenge a government or system just to pick a fight. This is not an archetype of street fighters or terrorists. Nobel Rebels respond to crimes against humanity and oppressive conditions that must be challenged for righteousness' sake. Gandhi, Martin Luther King, Jr., and Nelson Mandela are examples of well-known Noble Rebels who devoted their lives to liberating oppressed people. Gandhi perfected a style of rebellion known as nonviolent resistance that involved neither attacking nor returning aggression with aggression, while at the same time never yielding your position. People who believe in the power of force and the fist are not able to comprehend choices like nonviolent resistance that maneuver psychic and symbolic power. Though such choices appear to be powerless on the physical level, they are "archetypal tsunamis." Deriving their power from the symbolic realm, they take on universal meaning and purpose. Gandhi, King, and Mandela succeeded in their tasks not because they had more physical power, money, or armies on their side. They had none of that type of earthly support. These Noble Rebels succeeded because they became spiritual symbols of the revolutions they were leading. People understood that these men were taking on hardships so that the lives of many people could be better, not so that they themselves could become famous or wealthy.

Becoming a Noble Rebel is not a conscious decision. You are either born with this depth charge of an archetype in you or you're not. It's fair to ask, of course, "How do I know if I have the Nobel Rebel in me?" Well, how did Gandhi know he was passionate about helping liberate India from British rule, or Martin Luther King, Jr., know that he was passionate about working toward equality for all? These men were driven by an innate sense of justice for humanity, not just for themselves. Theirs was not a personal cause, though it cost them everything at the personal level of their life. But Noble Rebels are born passionate about human rights and human dignity, born to be servants of humanity. They are committed to humanity, whether or not they want to be. Trust me, if you have this impulse in you, you know it by now.

The Anarchist Rebel

The Anarchist is very likely the archetype most people associate with the Rebel. However, the Anarchist Rebel is more complex in motivation than what we see on television, which usually consists of Rebels toting guns or torching buildings. Anarchist Rebels should not be confused with Barbarian Rebels, who rampage through villages and turn children into heroin-addicted killing-soldiers. Unfortunately, we have become all too familiar with the Barbarian expression of the Rebel through conflicts in places like Rwanda and Darfur.

Although anarchy—political disorder—can and often does lead to barbaric chaos, the Anarchist Rebel is more often than not motivated to overthrow authority out of desperation. Often some spontaneous, cataclysmic event symbolic of that desperation unleashes a widespread belief that an opportunity for change has come. One example from recent history is the moment when Lech Walesa, founder of the Solidarity movement in Poland and later the country's first president, climbed a fence as an act of protest against the Soviet Union's orders to break up the workers' union. Immediately the union united behind Walesa, igniting a people's rebellion. The streets of Warsaw and other cities in Poland were in anarchy for weeks, but there was a purpose, a focus—freedom. The ultimate result was the end of the Cold War.

More recently, the events that took place in Tunisia in December 2010 ignited what is now referred to as the Arab Spring. A policewoman fined a simple vegetable seller named Mohamed Bouazizi for selling vegetables without a license and confiscated his cart. When he attempted to pay his $7 fine—a day's wages—she slapped him, spat in his face, and insulted his dead father. At the police station, where he went to plead his case, he was further humiliated. Stripped of his dignity and feeling complete helplessness and despair, Bouazizi set himself on fire as a final act of protest. To those witnessing his last act, Mohamed Bouazizi was a Noble Rebel standing up for the ultimate noble cause—human dignity.

Fighting broke out immediately. Ordinary citizens emerged as Anarchist Rebels, demanding an end to the repressive, abusive government that had long been in power in Tunisia. As usual when Anarchist Rebels hit the streets, buildings burn, riots ensue, and militant forces turn out in opposition. It wasn't long before the uprising in Tunisia spread to Egypt, then to Libya, then to Syria. It is important to note that social chaos was not the ultimate purpose of the Arab Spring. The common thread was the toppling of abusive dictatorships. Repressed people saw an opportunity to liberate themselves from decades of oppression by violent governments.

Not that there isn't a shadow side to the Anarchist Rebel. The sort of power this archetype wields is volatile. The Anarchist Rebel walks a thin line between fighting for the downfall of a repressive regime and taking advantage of that fight to strike out as a Barbarian Rebel. Both types of Rebels are driven by some of the darkest of human emotions, but if you're an Anarchist Rebel you have the precious element of hope for a better day as your driving force. If you take your eyes off that vision, however, it does not take much for the Barbarian to take over.

The Social/Civil Rebel

Social and civil rebellions are part of the fabric of many societies, and they give rise to the third type of Rebel. Though many such rebellions begin as protest movements, the underlying intention is to gather sufficient support around the issues to ignite a civil rebellion. The Suffragettes and the anti–Vietnam War protestors are perfect examples of Social/Civil Rebels who changed the course of American policy—and therefore history—because of their actions.

The groups behind the Tea Party and Occupy Wall Street are contemporary examples of Social/Civil Rebels representing a specific agenda or social argument filled with demands for change. If Social/ Civil Rebels garner enough support, the sounds of rebellion begin to stir within the masses. The Tea Party is a conservative grassroots movement that came together around political issues, including tax cuts and government spending. Tea Partiers succeeded in influencing election results in 2010 and remaining a presence in the 2012 presidential campaign.

The Occupy Wall Street group organized themselves around the disintegration of the middle class in America and the amassing of wealth by 1 percent of the American population. Occupy Wall

Street was heavily criticized for a lack of identifiable goals, mostly by mainstream media attempting to discredit the Occupy movement, but the key issues remained very much alive in the 2012 presidential campaign.

While many such rebellions come and go without making much of a dent in the social or political fabric, other movements led by Social/Civil Rebels have kept in check government actions that were covert or completely disregarded the rule of law and the Constitution. Investigative journalists who set up websites like MoveOn.org to expose news stories about the shadow side of government and Wall Street activities fall into this category. Social/Civil Rebels are the guard dogs of society that any government should rightly fear.

The Feminist Rebel

And now we come to the Feminist Rebel, whose activities are highlighted throughout the rest of this chapter, as this expression of the Rebel archetype is the most widespread and mainstream in our society at present. This trend could shift in the blink of an eye, however, and events in the world could draw the Anarchist and Social/Civil Rebels into the streets again. But the Feminist Rebel has adapted a more conventional avenue of expression, molding herself more in keeping with the grander social movement of individualism. Self-discovery and self-expression have had a profound impact on the form rebellion takes. Those of you with this archetype are more likely to be rebelling against conventional life choices than staging sit-ins.

Here are some ways in which Feminist Rebels are overturning convention: Marriage is losing ground as single-parent households increase. Divorce is now a viable choice for women, and no-fault divorce has removed the painful and humiliating need to prove adultery. Single women are choosing to adopt or bear children via sperm donors. The social climate has evolved dramatically since the most recent wave of Feminists took to the streets in the 1960s and 1970s. And as a society, we're turning inward, with more people engaged in self-exploration. If this is your archetype, you're part of the new wave of Rebels whose frontier is internal and whose rebellion is more likely to be against your inner boundaries than against any civil or social ones.

The contemporary Feminist Rebel archetype is new on the scene but carries threads of its historic elders while being very much of today's world. The Feminist Rebel's forebears carved a path—some with blood and guts—so that women could vote, have a voice in politics, work for equal pay (not to mention equal creative opportunities), and be sexually liberated. You may take all these rights for granted, but they didn't happen overnight.

The feminist movement has had three waves, each reflecting the issues of its day. The first wave was the women's suffrage movement, which culminated in the passage in 1920 of the 19th Amendment granting women the right to vote. Spearheaded by two Noble Rebels, Susan B. Anthony and Elizabeth Cady Stanton, these early feminists initiated a national movement of civil rebellion, awakening women to the reality that in a nation dedicated to equality and freedom, they had neither. These Noble Rebels, who were also Social/Civil Rebels, became the first Feminist Rebels, facing life threats and ferocious opposition. Women who joined in their efforts were arrested, beaten, hung by their thumbs, tortured, starved, and raped—all in American jails. But they did not give in.

The second wave of feminism was the Women's Liberation Movement, which began in the 1960s. Betty Friedan blew the doors off the American housewife's life with her now classic work, *The Feminine Mystique*. Friedan, a housewife and mother, challenged the social norm that those roles were enough to satisfy creative, dynamic, educated women. Journalist Gloria Steinem became the leading voice of the movement, whose members demanded reforms like job equality, sexual equality, and reproductive rights, and succeeded in tearing down social and civil barriers to women's rights.

There are many who deny that a third wave of feminism, starting in the 1980s and continuing to the present day, even exists. Women today live in a very different world from the one that prompted earlier social and political action. The contemporary Feminist Rebel is neither a radical nor a protestor. You are already living in a world that touts the values of diversity and individual expression. With the exception of those of you who have participated in the Occupy movement, you're probably not interested in fighting for a cause or even in being identified with one. Most of you with this archetype don't even identify with the word *feminist*. As a Feminist Rebel you're dynamic, unique, maybe unconventional, and even bold and daring, but definitely not a radical. You can even rebel against being a liberated woman if you want, and choose a traditional marriage-and-motherhood lifestyle or a hybrid that alternates careers with raising children. Back in the 1960s and 1970s, such a choice would have been considered a betrayal of everything the feminist movement stood for. Today's Feminist Rebel can engage her Rebel if she has to, but her expression of the archetype is far subtler than the other expressions of the Rebel we've explored.

The Feminist Rebel in you is far more likely to rebel against convention by selecting an edgy or offbeat outfit than to take a position on a current political issue. You're just not a fighter in the way Anarchist Rebels or Social/Civil Rebels once were. You have what it takes to get involved in social issues that touch a chord with you, but political and social issues don't define the Feminist Rebel archetype as they did many of its Rebel predecessors. You might, for example, be like Cornelia Guest, a famous debutante raised to be a society swan, who opted instead to hang out with Andy Warhol, become an animal rights advocate—she posed nude for a PETA ad—and start a vegan cookie company.

As a Feminist Rebel you cherish your self-confidence, your independence, and your willingness to take a risk. Should someone even consider tampering with these treasured personal freedoms, the Feminist Rebel in you has the grit to take the gloves off and start a personal if not professional rebellion. For Jill, a woman I know who perfectly fits the profile of the Feminist Rebel, the hot button is the notion *What will people think if you do that?* Jill operates in the world without the need for audience approval, which is a type of rebellion against one of the most common psychological roadblocks of all time. So many people postpone their lives out of fear of how the consequences of their choices will be viewed by others. Their fear of being humiliated should they fail or being ostracized if their choices threaten their nearest and dearest keeps them from taking a chance on living their dreams. Jill, however, rebelled against those constraints long ago, deciding that in order to be fulfilled, she needed to break away from concern with what others think about her life. Not surprisingly such a move required rebelling against the traditions she grew up with.

For another sort of Feminist Rebel, independence comes as a result of rebelling not against tradition but against her own rebellious nature. It begins with her involvement in a relationship with a controlling man. While she appears to be an independent woman who would never be bullied by anyone, behind closed doors she is living a nightmare in which her every move is controlled through criticism and perhaps physical abuse. At some level this Feminist Rebel is looking for a partner who will protect her, but in exchange for that, she yields her strength, her rebellious energy. That in turn erodes her self-respect, and so the cycle goes until the Feminist Rebel launches a rebellion to get out of the relationship entirely. A Feminist Rebel may unconsciously create an abusive relationship or work situation as a type of initiation into her authentic rebel qualities. If you've gone through a painful experience to recover your Rebel self and come out the other side, you know this truth firsthand.

Although the Feminist Rebel is the least rebellious of the Rebel Family in a classic sense, you can step into the Anarchist Rebel or the Social/Civil Rebel if necessary, because you have the potential in you. Many people have no idea that they have what it takes to engage in social rebellion because they have never been confronted with a worthy reason. Peaceful settings do not activate the Anarchist or Social/Civil Rebel in you. But if more and more of your civil rights were chipped away, at some point you would say, "Enough." You're a Feminist Rebel not because you were born to it, like the Noble Rebel, but because at some level you chose it.

Today's Feminist Rebel is a beneficiary of the devoted efforts of the women of the first and second wave who stood up for human rights believing we could make this world a better place. You may not man the barricades, but it's important for you to remember all the great women who paved the way for you to be something in this world, do something in this world, give something to this world. This is your heritage.

Unique Challenge

Since the end of the Vietnam War, we have resided in a society that has not been rebellion driven. The social and political freedoms gained in the 1960s and 1970s have been absorbed into the mainstream, and as a society we've moved from rebellion in the streets to rebellion in the spirit. So how does this shift in the social climate influence an archetype like the Feminist Rebel? Well, the archetype evolves into another expression in keeping with the thinking patterns of the collective social mind.

Breaking with convention and being experimental in fashion or lifestyle choices is one expression of the individualist movement that emerged out of the rebellious era of the 1960s. For Feminist Rebels today, what you wear and how you live are the main ways in which you represent your independence. Personal style, as we discovered with the Fashionista archetype, can be a visible statement of power.

As a Feminist Rebel, you thrive on pushing the envelope and sometimes on sending shock waves into the social atmosphere with the choices you make in everything from hair color to motherhood.

All Rebels, including the Feminist Rebel, are change agents by archetypal design. Traditional ways of doing things make you feel as if you're being smothered. You can probably relate to those young teens telling their moms, "It's so unfair that you won't let me get a tattoo," because that was you just a few years ago. Now it's likely you have a tattoo or two, along with Feminist Rebels like Angelina Jolie, Rihanna, Christina Ricci, Victoria Beckham, and even Helen Mirren.

The challenge for you is to discover a creative, dynamic, and—this is important—*productive* way to utilize your rebellious nature lest it become a destructive element in your psyche. Fields where your vitality and convention-busting urges are ideal include music, the arts, fashion, design, cosmetics, and the tech arena, as the creed common to people in these areas is *Why not—and what else can we do?* But even if you're drawn to more conventional fields like law, social work, and investigative journalism—justice is the grace of your archetype—your Feminist Rebel has more than enough guts to compete and succeed.

Universal Lesson

No matter which type of Rebel you are, restraint is probably not your strong suit. The Rebel archetype has a reputation for having a hair-trigger temper, for overreacting, and for not thinking decisions all the way through to their consequences. The universal lesson, therefore, for all you Rebels is to learn that even "rebellious" decisions are best made thoughtfully and carefully. That requires knowing the difference between rebellious *reactions* and conscious rebellious *decisions*. Both have consequences, and those consequences can be hurt feelings and even chaos if you hurtle into a situation reactively.

Rebellious reactions by definition aren't thought through from beginning to end. They tend to be emotionally charged and careless; frequently, they're power statements that erupt out of frustration but lack focus, leadership, and a clear outcome, raising questions like: What are the specific plans for after the rebellion? Who will be in charge? Where do you go from here? Starting fires is easy. Containing them is a different challenge. And as we all know, if a fire gets out of control, entire neighborhoods can go up in flames.

The same can be said about starting rebellions of even the mildest sort in your own life. Every choice you make sets some cycle of change into motion, but this is all the more crucial to remember when the choices you're making affect the comfort zones of other people. Rebels, even Feminist Rebels, are notorious for breaking through others' comfort zones.

So the lesson for this archetype is: Don't rebel just to make noise. When it comes to making decisions, especially those that initiate change and shatter the rules of convention, it's essential to call upon the best of your inner spirit to take charge. If you are going to launch a rebellion, reflect on this: *I know what I don't want. Do I know what I do want? Is it worth a rebellion or does this situation just call for a discussion?*

Defining Grace: Justice

The grace of justice serves the Rebel archetype, as the Rebel inherently rises against injustice and oppression of any sort. The Rebel also inspires others to break through barriers and initiate new beginnings because it's the right choice. Like all graces, justice has many expressions. At the ground level, justice is associated with legal justice, with what takes place in the courtroom. Many a rebellion has been set into motion for lack of legal justice in a society. Thanks to American Rebels, the scripting of our Bill of Rights assured that the United States would be a nation based upon the rule of law and justice.

On a more subtle level, this grace inspires the Rebel in you to be a change agent in less aggressive ways, always moving in the direction of introducing the new. Rebels are the people who challenge outdated social codes and mores, lending support to issues like gay marriage and medical marijuana because you view them as matters of civil justice. When Rebels get behind issues, politicians pay attention, as evidenced by the number of states that now sanction marriage between same-sex couples.

As a Feminist Rebel, you can easily find yourself drawn to support a human rights cause simply because you believe it's the right thing to do. You may not be a political or social activist in a conventional sense, but when it comes to what's fair and just in life, you are right there, speaking out.

Inner Shadow

The dark side of the Feminist Rebel's independent streak and unconventional thinking is your personal agenda—a craving for attention. But, you might ask, who doesn't have a personal agenda most of the time? Let's be honest: that's how we humans are wired. But when it comes to the Feminist Rebel, attention and appreciation are actual agenda items for you. Your Feminist Rebel craves recognition because you need to feel a sense of accomplishment. After all, if you're going to go to all that effort to be different, unique, daring, and bold in the world, someone should at least notice, right? But what if that doesn't happen? What if all your efforts to be a rule breaker fall flat? Or what if another Feminist Rebel is even more outrageous than you, eclipsing your originality? All I can say is: Look out.

As a Feminist Rebel, you're creative, ambitious, dynamic, fun, even wild. But when you're not appreciated for your outrageousness, you can flush red with jealousy and reshape the world into a battlefield, turning friends into competitors if not deadly enemies. You ignite a rebellion in your mind, imagining what you would say to this person or that. Instead of a brainstorm, you have storms in the brain—sometimes resulting in actual migraine headaches—until you come to your senses.

Personal agendas can become dangerous personal itineraries, no matter what archetype we're dealing with. For the Feminist Rebel, however, it's particularly important to satisfy your own need for recognition and not look to others to do it for you. And when an attack of jealousy strikes, I suggest you find some place to cool down lest you start a fire by reacting to your own dark brain storms. You're always up to something, so whatever else you do, be honest with yourself about your private agendas. You'll thank yourself for it one day.

Male Counterpart

Everything I've said about the Rebel archetype, except for the Feminist Rebel, applies equally to men and women. But there's one

Rebel male who has become particularly noteworthy for bringing out the Caregiver/Rescuer in women everywhere. I'm speaking of the dark, misunderstood, Bad-boy Rebel, famously made into an icon by James Dean in the 1955 film *Rebel Without a Cause*. Dean introduced this male Rebel to the American public, and women immediately gravitated to the archetype, believing they were the answer to his pain. Dean's character, Jim Stark, embodies the Rebel who suffers for reasons he can't articulate. Why is Jim so morose? He comes from a typical middle-class, suburban family, yet something is amiss. The archetypal roles in the home are switched: the controlling mother dominates her husband and son. The teen lacks a strong male role model, and he desperately wants one. He is in a power crisis. His father is unable to initiate him into manhood, as fathers are meant to do. Jim's only way to express his despair at entering manhood as a powerless man is by rebelling, acting out his frustration in the world around him.

Myth of the Rebel

Prometheus, one of the Titans in Greek mythology, gives us a myth of the Rebel archetype. Zeus, in order to keep mere mortals from getting too powerful, refused to give them the element of fire. Prometheus, however, rebelled and stole fire from Zeus, giving it to men who dwelled in caves; with fire, they flourished. Zeus was furious and ordered Prometheus to be hung upside down from a cliff, so that he could be tortured during the day by an eagle that ate his liver, which then grew back during the night so that his torment could be repeated again the next day.

After the fire debacle, Zeus decided to send mortals a gift that would remind them in no uncertain terms who held the power in the world. He ordered his goddesses to fashion a goddess who would be beautiful and seductive but above all curious. That was Pandora.

Zeus sent Pandora to earth to marry Epimetheus, Prometheus's brother. As a wedding present, Zeus gave Pandora a jar—in some versions of the myth it's a box—with strict orders never to open it.

But as Zeus knew she would, Pandora couldn't wait to see what was inside. Slipping away from her husband, she hurried to her room and slid the lid off the jar. Out flew all the sufferings destined to plague mankind: illness, tragedy, death, grief, envy, hatred, and so on. Pandora tried to put the lid back on the jar, but it was too late. Distraught, she took one last look inside, and there at the bottom lay one more gift: hope.

The moral here is open for discussion, as all great myths invite dialogue. But certainly one interpretation is that challenging the wisdom of the gods is a mistake that carries severe consequences. Yet the gods remain compassionate, as even the consequences humanity must face are buffered with hope. Prometheus, assuming that Zeus would never give man fire, rebelled against the wisdom of the gods and took it upon himself to redirect the cosmic plan. He paid a serious price for his act of rebellion. And yet the gift of hope suggests that Zeus understood that Prometheus's intentions were good, that he had wanted to give human beings fire to help in their development, not to harm them.

Prometheus remains a powerful symbol of the Rebel because we are always rebelling against the gods in our lives, thinking that we know best. In other words, we go against our own intuition or inner guidance. And what is the source of our guidance if not divinely inspired wisdom?

Lifestyle Challenge

For the Feminist Rebel, the challenge is to be prepared for how your life will change as a result of rebellious choices. Don't assume that *rebellious* refers only to a choice with attitude. You're not necessarily thumbing your nose at the world. A rebellious choice can be anything from deciding to wear a daring new fashion style to pursuing a spiritual practice that represents breaking from the tradition you grew up in. What a rebellious choice does is change your life in some way. You may think that the decision to wear something a bit more daring isn't all that rebellious, especially if you don't get the reaction you anticipated—everyone sitting up and taking notice, for example. It's your inner reaction that actually matters more than any social waves you may set in motion by your behavior. Rebellious choices take courage, and they feel liberating, as if you have just parachuted from an airplane. And in a sense, you have—psychologically at least—when you shed an old pattern that strongly influenced your choices up to that point.

Once you break free of one pattern, breaking free of the next and the one after that gets easier and easier. Many women I've met who have rebelled from traditional roles talk about the dual feeling of exhilaration and fear they experience when they realize they no longer fit into the restricted life they've led, yet they're unsure of how to navigate in the world as a more independent woman. They've awakened the Feminist Rebel in themselves, albeit with a whispering voice, but it's there, and for these women that part of themselves is their most thrilling archetypal discovery.

Recognize Your Archetype: Are You a Rebel?

Rebels usually recognize themselves for what they are. But just in case you're still unsure if you fit this archetype, take a look at the list of behavior patterns and characteristics on the next page and see if you relate to them. Regardless of which style of Rebel you are—Noble, Anarchist, Social/Civil, or Feminist—the general characteristics will apply to you.

- You've shown a rebellious streak since childhood.

- You define your character by your right to challenge injustice.

- You speak out against discrimination and oppression.

- You resist taking orders and follow your own counsel.

- You're pursuing a different spiritual path from the faith of your childhood.

- You thrive on making waves and upsetting the status quo.

- You are unconventional and independent, a free and creative thinker.

- You would have led a rebel charge in the American Revolution if you had been around back then.

- You do things in nontraditional ways.

- You're an agent of change introducing radically new ideas into the culture.

- You wear bold and daring styles.

- You choose the less-traveled road.

Step into Your Archetype:
Tapping into the Power of the Rebel

Once you define yourself as a Rebel, what then? How can you harness all that rebellious energy to bring about positive change in the world? Here are some suggestions to help you work your archetype to full advantage:

- **Break free.** If you've been keeping your Rebel under wraps, it's time to let her loose. Whatever issue you feel strongly about—unfair practices, gay rights, food safety, suppression of free speech—take a stand. It's essential to bring the issue into the open and set an agenda for change. Then, to make sure you can achieve your goals, rally the troops. Round up others who are moved to action by the same concerns.

- **Contain yourself.** Rebels tend to be hotheads. You can sabotage your best efforts if you act rashly or shoot your mouth off. Learn to take a few beats and think through the consequences before you jump into action or say something you can't take back.

- **Be a Rebel with a cause.** There's a difference between conscious rebellion and just being reactive. Make sure that your urge to topple existing structures has a legitimate purpose and isn't just target practice. Sometimes the most effective way to bring about change is gradual. Try a "soft" rebellion: be strategic and have a plan. Slow and steady may bring more people on board.

- **Dress for the (inner) revolution.** Perhaps you're not cut out for protest marches. Your form of rebellion might be dyeing your hair pink, getting a tattoo, or trading your "safe" wardrobe for one that would put club kids to shame. Go ahead, do it. Don't be shy. One little act of liberation leads to another. Pretty soon you won't be living your life to gain others' approval.

- **Raise a Rebel.** Sure, teenagers are rebellious; the teens are all about fighting for independence. But what about your other little Rebels, from preschool age to junior high? Should you encourage or quash a rebellious streak in them? If it's just childish stubbornness or a test of your authority, no, don't indulge it. But if you sense you have a freethinker in the making, be supportive. Let your mini-Rebel swim against the tide, wear crazy clothes, eat dinner for breakfast. Next thing you know, she might be rallying her schoolmates to call for healthier lunches or leading a demonstration against unfair hiring at the mall.

Power is a Rebel's best friend, the engine of positive change. But you need to know how to get it, keep it, and use it wisely—and figure out what to do when you lose it. Here are some strategies for working with power:

Where You Gain Power

- **Expressing yourself.** You need to be free to be you, even to be outrageous at times.

- **Making the most of your feminine power.** Women have worked hard for equal rights. Don't take those freedoms for granted; enjoy them fully.

- **Taking risks and living boldly.** "Shy Rebel" is a contradiction in terms. Go for it.

- **Championing the rights of others.** You're at your best speaking out against discrimination and repression.

• **Fighting a big fight.** Don't waste energy pursuing your own agenda. Take on a worthy issue that's bigger than your personal concerns.

Where You Lose Power (and how to regain it)

• **Overreacting or acting impulsively.** Recklessness can damage your cause. Practice yoga or meditation to cool down.

• **Losing your temper.** Same thing.

• **Letting desperation drive your actions.** You'll get better results if you have clear objectives. Effective campaigns have a platform.

• **Rebelling just for the sake of rebelling.** Channel that energy into something constructive. Surely you can find a worthy cause.

• **Ignoring your inner Rebel.** Repressing the urge isn't the solution either. Find a positive outlet.

• **Throwing a fit when you don't get recognition.** So you rebelled and nobody applauded? Applaud yourself.

• **Failing to see how your rebellious acts affect others.** Revolutions have consequences, usually big ones. Be mindful of what you're doing every step of the way.

Checklist for the Rebel

☐ I can work out my rebellious urges by experimenting with my fashion and lifestyle choices.

☐ I appreciate the freedoms I enjoy as a woman today and am grateful to the Rebels whose courage and dedication made them possible.

☐ I will stand up to any individual, organization, or government that tries to limit rights—my own or anyone else's.

☐ I'm committed to being a responsible Rebel. I think through any social or political action I wish to take, to make sure it will help, not harm.

☐ I calm my angry mind with the Buddha's words: "Hatred never ceases by hatred, but by love alone is healed."

Final Thoughts

The Rebel archetype carries your fire, your power. Get to know this part of yourself. It takes great courage to stand up for what you believe, but it's exactly that type of courage that gives life true purpose and meaning.

CHAPTER 11

The Spiritual Seeker

Archetype Family: *Spiritual*

Other Expressions: *Mystic, Healer*

Life Journey: *To become a spiritually congruent human being*

Unique Challenge: *To create a life that blends your spiritual, emotional, and physical needs*

Universal Lesson: *Truth will set you free.*

Defining Grace: *Humility*

Inner Shadow: *The ordinary rules of life do not apply to me because I'm spiritual and therefore special. Nothing bad will happen to me because I'm on a spiritual path.*

Male Counterpart: *Spiritual Seeker*

Myth of the Spiritual Seeker: *Following a spiritual path will lead to poverty and loneliness.*

Behavior Patterns and Characteristics: *The Spiritual Seeker . . .*

- *trusts intuition unconditionally.*
- *seeks insight into who she really is.*
- *searches for the true meaning and purpose of her life.*
- *is committed to a path of spiritual evolution.*
- *gives priority to spiritual understanding.*
- *wants more out of life than material success.*

Lifestyle Challenge: *Awakening your intuitive intelligence*

Life Journey

As much as the world around us has changed over the past 50 years, as much if not more has shifted within us. We're now becoming an inward-driven society as well as an externally ambitious one. We've developed an appetite for understanding the nature of the psyche and the spirit and for listening to intuitive intelligence. We're asking questions about the meaning of life—and the purpose of our own lives. We have become seekers of spiritual data of all kinds.

Most people think of a Mystic as someone living a committed spiritual or monastic lifestyle. But the counterculture of the '60s and the New Age movement initiated a shift that has redefined the face of American spirituality and given form and function to another archetype, the Spiritual Seeker. Breaking free from the restrictions of traditional religion, Seekers are devouring books on Eastern religions, exploring meditation, and increasingly turning to holistic health care, which has brought a spiritual dimension to healing. The contemporary Mystic has evolved into the Spiritual Seeker/ Mystic, a hybrid archetype that blends the rich interior nature of the Mystic with the modern values of the Spiritual Seeker, merging what is eternal about the human spirit with what is essential to the times we live in. Together, these two archetypes are redefining the essence of the spiritual path.

In the world today, the new monastery is the global village itself, a sacred field of life we must all work to sustain. Therefore, the Spiritual Seeker, with its inclination toward the external world, is perfect partnered with the Mystic, the archetype that governs the activities of your inner being. Your Spiritual Seeker prefers the ego-based world, and your Mystic is drawn to all that is eternal about you.

But what characterizes each of these archetypes—the Spiritual Seeker, the Mystic, and the Spiritual Seeker/Mystic? And if the spiritual life is calling to you in some way, where do you fall on the spectrum between them?

The Spiritual Seeker

For some of you, it might have been a personal crisis or a health crisis that drew you into a bookstore to pick up your first self-help book or prompted you to attend your first lecture on human consciousness or spirituality. For others, it might have been a fleeting experience of intuitive intelligence or a moment of transcendent clarity that suggested there is more to this world than meets the eye. The Spiritual Seeker archetype came into being as people like you became curious about the nonmaterial world. And this archetype has continued to increase its gravitational field as unrest and uncertainty in the world have led more and more of us to look for "the still point of the turning world," as the poet T. S. Eliot put it.

Notice, however, that the name of this archetype is Spiritual *Seeker*, not Spiritual *Finder*. A Spiritual Seeker is, by definition, always looking for something more. But more what? That *more* question generally presents itself in the guise of some kind of disruption in your life. Something unexpected happens, and suddenly you're standing at a crossroads. Perhaps the challenge is a divorce or financial difficulties or a tragic loss or a serious health diagnosis, but whatever it is, the result is that suddenly the life path you have been following no longer seems viable. If you are like most people with the Spiritual Seeker archetype, it is at this point that you begin to think, perhaps for the first time, *What is the meaning and purpose of my life? There has to be more than what has been driving me up to now.*

The truth is, *What is the meaning and purpose of my life?* is not so much a question as an invocation, a prayer, in which you are asking to be shown a deeper and more authentic life that you could be living. You are asking to have the life your ego created replaced by the life you are capable of living as a more conscious individual. The Tibetan Buddhist teacher Chögyam Trungpa Rinpoche famously cautioned his students, "My advice to you is not to undertake the spiritual path. It is too difficult, too long, and too demanding . . . However, if you do begin, it is best to finish."

Centuries ago, monks and nuns would prepare for years to ask *For what purpose was I born?* They understood that uttering this powerful invocation was like saying, "Strip away the illusions from my life. Let me see who I am clearly, my dark side and my light. Give me the courage to love deeply and to challenge the part of me that has the power to destroy other human beings."

For what purpose were *you* born? Your ego would probably love the answer to be a glamorous job or the perfect marriage or fulfillment of some other dream, but the truth is that meaning and purpose are mystical forces, not commercial ones. Meaning and purpose are never just *given* to us. Rather, these gifts begin to pulsate in your soul as a result of accepting a path of service through which you discover your innate abilities to make life better for others as well as for yourself. Fears that a spiritual path will leave you homeless or poor or lonely are ever so common. Nonetheless they are simply nightmares of the ego, based on illusion. But these are strong nightmares, powerful enough to keep some Spiritual Seekers seeking a path of meaning and purpose that offers material rewards, until a crisis of some sort intervenes, awakening the need to look for answers within.

The Mystic

The Mystic is the oldest, most complex, and in many ways most intriguing member of the Meditative family. The Mystic archetype is like a prism with many facets. It cannot be captured in a single, overarching definition because it makes itself known to each individual through personal inner experience. The Mystic has been awakened to her inner guidance and trusts it implicitly. Trungpa Rinpoche used to tell students "First thought, best thought." This makes perfect sense to a Mystic: you instinctively respond to the lightning-fast hits of intuition that are your fundamental way of knowing.

In most of us, once guidance has filtered into the mind from the pure air of the soul, it gets lost in the chaotic control patterns of our fears and insecurities and the illusions of our five senses, which reduce us to trusting what we can see, hear, taste, smell, and feel over our inner knowledge of the truth. A Mystic, however, has awakened to the authority of her inner senses and consciously works to withdraw from the illusions of the mental and physical world. That does not mean you always achieve this. As a Mystic you confront the same life issues as any human being. What the mystical path or mystical consciousness offers, however, is a sense of authentic inner truth about what is real and what is not real in life.

Mystical experiences are not unique to the Mystic either. We've all had moments in which we were lifted outside time and space and into the vast domain of higher consciousness. But Mystics seem to engage with life primarily from the vantage point of this expanded consciousness. You are not afraid of how encounters with truth will change your life; in fact, you seek truth instead of running from it. From poets like Maya Angelou to scientists like Albert Einstein and Stephen Hawking to astronauts like Edgar Mitchell, people with the Mystic archetype have broken through the barriers of ordinary fear-based thinking and awakened their intuitive intellect. For these individuals, as for so many mystics, fulfilling work dedicated to the betterment of humankind is a stepping-stone to truth.

The Spiritual Seeker/Mystic

The union of the contemporary Spiritual Seeker and the classic Mystic has come about because we require both for spiritual practice in today's world. It's not enough to continue seeking but never really change your life, never really challenge your inner values, never really learn to walk humbly on sacred ground. And yet we live in a world that no longer accommodates monastics. Few are called to retreat into devoted lives of prayer and silence within the protected walls of monasteries and ashrams. At the same time, we are asking ourselves profound, soul-sized questions that awaken the Mystic within us. Not content with simply wondering how to be happy, nearly every Spiritual Seeker one day asks the significant questions that shatter the boundaries between the ego and the soul. If you have the Spiritual Seeker archetype but that moment hasn't come yet, don't worry—it will.

The Life Journey of the Spiritual Seeker/Mystic centers on a commitment to live in conscious union of body, mind, and spirit. The adage *Walk your talk* could well be the mantra of this archetype, as a congruent person is dedicated to living in harmony with truth. A congruent person doesn't say one thing and mean another, or compromise her integrity by denying her feelings. Congruence demands that how you feel and what you believe be aligned. Living in harmony with truth means you are not harboring secrets or hiding behind old wounds, not betraying yourself or others. Becoming congruent does not happen overnight, however. It isn't the payoff for a weekend workshop. It is a lifelong journey, a lifetime commitment.

The Spiritual Seeker/Mystic is the perfect archetype to support the Life Journey of becoming a congruent individual. The Spiritual Seeker in you is drawn to knowing more about why you are the way you are and to helping you solve such mysteries of your inner life as *What am I really looking for?* and *What truly makes me happy?* These types of questions often initiate the spiritual journey. Underneath the surface quest for another job or something else you think will make you happy is the ever-present pulsating force of the Mystic, drawing you deeper on the path of personal truth. Eventually the Spiritual Seeker in you acknowledges your inner Mystic, who reminds you through your intuition that you can only find lasting happiness when you have the courage to be honest with yourself about who you are, what you feel, what you believe, and how you want to live your life.

Unique Challenge

The question for today's Spiritual Seeker is where you intend to position matters of the spirit among your other life interests and values. Is your spiritual path a hobby, an intellectual interest, or a true devotion? We are a society that prefers reason to the mystical realm. We need proof before we leap, and often we would rather discuss the type of god we want over dinner than risk having an authentic mystical experience through prayer and reflection. We are drawn to spiritual literature but terrified of spiritual experiences. We are intrigued by the skills and gifts of the spirit, such as intuitive intelligence and the grace of healing, but we generally think of prayer as an SOS. How many times have we heard a doctor say, "I've done all I can for this patient. Now all we can do is pray." What he means is, *Now that medical science has worked its wonders, go ahead and see if there's any cosmic force that can help out.* If we really acknowledged the power of prayer, of course, we would pray before beginning a medical procedure—and with all attending medical staff beside us. But that's in an ideal world.

Over the years I've encountered every sort of spiritual person, from those I consider genuine Mystics to others who ask me, "Can you suggest any prayers that actually *work*?" Translation: *Got any magic up your sleeve?* During a break in a workshop I was giving on prayer and healing, I talked with a participant about what she was seeking from her spiritual life. Her face went blank for a moment before she finally responded, "Happiness. I just want to be happy." Happy? So I asked her what "happy" meant for her—what would she have to be given in order for her to be happy? "Security and a partner," she replied.

In another workshop with about 800 participants, I tossed out three questions: *Do you consider yourselves to be on a spiritual path? What are you seeking from your spiritual path? Is your spiritual life a priority for you or a hobby?* Most people considered themselves to be on a spiritual path—no surprise there. But it was apparent from the responses to the second question that few had ever asked themselves, "What *am* I seeking? What is it that I'm actually pursuing by reading all these books and attending all these lectures? What am I really doing here?"

I then asked them, "How many of you have at least 20 books on spirituality or related subjects in your library?" Nearly all raised their hands. Then I asked, "How many of you would purchase 20 books on any other subject, even though you had no idea why you were reading them?" Laughter broke out as I suggested that they were deliberately clouding their minds—choosing to remain in their intellects as a way of avoiding actually encountering the interior self and their true spiritual path. I mentioned the woman who was on her spiritual path to find security and a partner, and several people admitted that their motivations were much the same: financial security, a life partner, assurance that they wouldn't fail, and good health.

So I concluded that many Spiritual Seekers today think of the spiritual path as a route to life health, happiness, and security. The glitch with this archetypal road map is that these goals are not, and never have been, the core goals of an authentic spiritual path. They are more in keeping with what we want out of everyday life—the generic goals for material and emotional contentment. And mind you, that's fine. These are basic survival needs that every human being requires in order to feel grounded.

But they are not the directives of a spiritual path. Rather, a spiritual path focuses you inward, to discover your interior qualities and confront your inner obstacles. You turn to your spiritual self in order to come into alignment with your values, your beliefs, and your core truths. As an example, ask yourself this question: "How much of my life is controlled by my fear of being humiliated?" That is a core spiritual question that takes you deep into your being. Turning you inside out, such a question beckons you to begin a spiritual self-examination in which you truly observe how and why you make the decisions you do. How much authority does the fear of being humiliated have over you? If you were to challenge this fear, how would your life change? Would you listen differently to your inner guidance if you developed a stronger sense of self-esteem? The spiritual path is a rigorous journey, one that takes the rest of your life. The goal is the liberation of your spirit—of your capacity to love without fear and receive love and to rise to your fullest creative potential.

So if the Spiritual Seeker is your archetype, your path is going deeper within and discovering the many reasons for which you were given life, and then having the courage to explore your gifts and talents. If you're one of those people, however, who worries that if you follow such a path, you'll be required to give away all your money or give up sex for a celibate life, then rest assured that those are outdated fears. We're not still living in the Middle Ages.

It's true, however, that historically the spiritual path was viewed as separate from life in the physical world. There was God's domain, and there was the human domain, each with its own set of rules. We were taught that if we're good and obey God, then nothing bad will happen to us because God is a just god who protects good people. Except that it doesn't really work out like that. In reality, bad things happen to good people and good things happen to bad people. Life isn't fair. Understanding this is an essential step on your spiritual path. Instead of searching for the life you want, you now seek to understand life as it is. As a true Spiritual Seeker/Mystic, you search for truth about the journey of life, pursuing such questions as *How does the divine make itself known to us? What is the order of life really about? If there is no logical order, then how do I know what signs to follow on the road of my life?*

The nature of the divine is best understood through studying what is consistent, governs all life, and transcends all religions—namely the mystical laws of the universe. When you turn your attention to how the mystical laws work within your every breath, the Spiritual Seeker in you merges with your inner Mystic.

Consider, for example, the law that says *Every cause generates an effect.* Applied to your personal life, it means that every choice you make has a consequence. The consequences of your choices, no matter how minute or grand, eventually find their way into the details of your daily life. A comment made in haste to someone today may well come back to haunt you ten years from now, while an act of kindness you've long forgotten may end up being the reason a loan officer saves your home from foreclosure—which actually happened to a man I know.

Yet another mystical law teaches us *What is in one is in the whole.* Consider the impact a single person's actions can have on the whole world. One terrorist, Osama bin Laden, in triggering the events of 9/11 changed the safety of the global village forever, and with it the future destiny of every single human being on the planet.

This same law also works in a beneficial way when it comes to how all of humanity benefits from your individual acts of kindness, generosity, love, forgiveness, and prayer. This is a mystical truth, so it is impossible to confirm such a statement. Great Mystics such as Francis of Assisi, Teresa of Ávila, and Rumi wrote at length about their inner experiences of these mystical laws, but the only way they could reveal these truths to others was through the courageous choices they made in their lives. You can do the same.

Universal Lesson

Let's return to the question *As a Spiritual Seeker, what are you really seeking?* If I told you that you're really seeking a way to become comfortable with truth, what would you say? If you reflect on the impulses that compel you to continue on a spiritual path, always seeking some new thought or idea, you would ultimately realize that you are searching for a way to become sufficiently empowered so that you're no longer intimidated by truth. One of the greatest sources of personal suffering is self-betrayal—feeling or thinking one way but acting another, with the full awareness that you're going against yourself. Many people live in an endless cycle of small and large acts of self-betrayal, from remaining in dysfunctional marriages to feeling they can't speak openly about their feelings to even the people closest to them. The thought of uttering one truthful sentence is intimidating, because they know that truth holds the power to shatter a lifetime built on lies and illusions. The lesson then for the Spiritual Seeker is to truly grasp that the truth will set you free.

We make up all sorts of excuses for why we avoid speaking the truth: *I don't want to hurt anyone; I don't know what will happen to me; I just want to keep peace in the family.* Whatever the excuse, the result is the same: choosing a life of self-betrayal because it feels safe. We say we want things to change, but when it comes down to it, we resist because it's too scary.

Truth, however, is a change agent. One potent truthful sentence can, and often does, shift the direction of your life. Think *I'm not happy here,* or *I'm in love with someone else,* and your old life is over. One of the ways we betray ourselves is by putting more effort into avoiding the truth than in empowering ourselves to hear it and be guided by it. And that's unfortunate because all of us, regardless of archetype, have an inborn desire to free ourselves from hiding behind deceit or compromising ourselves in order to feel safe. We think wealth and fame will finally give us the power to speak the truth, but it ends up burdening us more. How many times have we heard people who've lost everything say, "I'm finally free"?

It is impossible to live a congruent life unless you are truthful with yourself. Otherwise, your mind will be filled with one agenda and your heart with another. If you're uncomfortable with truth you can't rely on yourself to be consistent or to keep your word. Learning to be comfortable with your inner truth is fundamental to the health of your body, mind, and spirit. The lesson for the Spiritual Seeker is that truth will set you free.

Defining Grace: Humility

The word *humility* can be off-putting, as to most people, it suggests a condition of powerlessness, poverty, and defeat. A humble person, in this view, has no alternative but to acquiesce in all matters of significance, for they come to the table with no power whatsoever. But humility isn't like that at all. Simply stated, it's the grace that prevents you from harming yourself or others because of your pride, greed, anger, or arrogance. Humility is a protective shield: it speaks to you as a soft voice in the midst of the worst arguments, asking you, "Are you sure you want to say such cruel words to this person? If you do, you might win the moment but lose the friendship forever." Humility is the grace that tells you to walk out of the room and cool off before you say or do something you'll regret, and only to walk back in when you've calmed down.

You've probably been saved from more disasters than you can count by this grace. Though you might have felt defeated in the moment, how grateful you were later on when you thought about the damage you might have done had you not heeded that warning voice that seemed to come out of nowhere, cautioning you to turn down the volume on your anger or pride.

The problem for most of us is that we make no distinction between the power of humility and the fear of being humiliated. Humility and humiliation are as different as night and day. True humility allows you to move freely through the world, knowing you won't do harm. Fear of being humiliated, on the other hand, is a prison that controls your every thought and every action. Many people spend an entire lifetime never feeling free to take a single risk or make one outrageous choice, out of fear of being humiliated.

Protecting yourself against being humiliated is all consuming. It saps creative energy you could be investing in becoming a better person or doing great things in the world or even just enjoying simple pleasures like gardening or making love. You are completely at the mercy of your survival-oriented reptilian brain, as it continually spews out paranoid thoughts that poison your relations with others.

Humility allows you to reenter the circle of humanity. No longer bound by the fear of humiliation, you are able to realize the truth that we are all sharing the same Life Journey.

Inner Shadow

The shadow side of the Spiritual Seeker is rooted in spiritual arrogance, in believing that you are special because you lead a spiritual life. The corollary to that is the belief that being spiritually special protects you against the slings and arrows of life that ordinary people suffer. I've heard people who are caught in the shadow side of this archetype say, "I can't believe this happened to me, because I eat all the right foods and meditate and do yoga." And so? Should organic food protect you from a car accident? Or bunions?

This kind of thinking isn't new. It is an echo of the age-old belief that the spiritually dedicated are not subject to the ordinary laws of life here on Earth. Inevitably, of course, this attitude leads to disappointment, as you discover that no matter how careful you are, no matter how much prayer and meditation you do, you continue to age just as all living beings do, and the realities of life keep coming up for you, just as they do for everyone else. The role of spiritual practice is not to give you the ability to transcend the natural order of life but rather to help you learn how to flow with it.

Male Counterpart

There is no essential difference between men and women in how the Spiritual Seeker archetype is expressed. Men are as attracted to a search for meaning and purpose as women. Gender has nothing to do with our yearning for a spiritual life.

That said, women make up the greater percentage of spiritually oriented people in our society today. They buy the most books and fill the vast majority of seats at conferences and lectures in the human consciousness field. (If there's anywhere men outnumber women, it might be in a Zen meditation hall. Zen's samurai tradition still lends a macho aura to the practice, but even that is changing as Zen adapts to American life.) But by and large, if there is no essential difference in the core spirituality of the sexes, it's fair to ask, "Where are the men at all these spiritual events? And why aren't more men buying books on spirituality and personal development?"

The answer is as logical as logic itself. As a society, we still associate the spiritual path with sacrifice and poverty. So when men peer through the window of anything spiritual—or "woo-woo," as many like to say—they balk at entering for fear their wallets will evaporate out of their trouser pockets. With profit and power viewed as anathema to the spiritual path, how could a man feel safe seeking spiritual awakening while working as a Wall Street banker?

That said, the archetypal pattern of Right Livelihood—of choosing work that is congruent with our inner values and not harmful to the planet—is gradually taking shape in the world, offering men as well as women a way to envision themselves as simultaneously successful and spiritual, rather than having to choose one or the other as a life path. But mainstream acceptance of this ethos is a way off. Until we as a society close the divide between body and soul, mind and heart, reason and intuition, men will view the domain of the spiritual as feminine territory and the earth as theirs to rule.

The one place that men are finding a comfort zone is in the yoga community, but that is largely because yoga is viewed in the West as physical exercise rather than spiritual practice. Only a handful of the millions of men and women practicing yoga in America have any interest in undertaking it as a way of establishing a relationship with the sacred.

Myth of the Spiritual Seeker

The myth of the Spiritual Seeker archetype is that the spiritual path leads to poverty and loneliness. As I've tried to reassure you, that's simply a carryover from age-old religious views that divided heaven and earth, body and soul, and pretty much said that whatever falls on the earthly side of the equation is a one-way ticket to unhappiness and ruin. There was no middle ground for our Christian forefathers, who took to heart the teaching that it's harder for a rich person to get into heaven than for a camel to go through the eye of a needle, and counted poverty among the highest virtues.

It was no stretch then to believe that deprivation awaited anyone who sought a spiritual life. What's more, for centuries poverty *was* the general lot for all but the very rich, so viewing your suffering as a spiritual journey gave meaning and dignity to a daily existence that was, as Thomas Hobbes put it, "solitary, poor, nasty, brutish, and short."

Amazingly, however, those century-old superstitions and social undercurrents persist to this day. A surprising number of people find it difficult to charge an adequate fee for their services because they work in what's considered a spiritual profession, such as spiritual direction, massage therapy, or teaching meditation. Then, too, it is often their clients who balk at paying fees on the grounds that spiritual teachings should be freely given. "If I was an attorney or a CEO, no one would balk at me earning a six-figure salary," one woman told me. "But because I do spiritual counseling, people expect me to charge what they can afford, and not what I need to earn." Even people whose jobs have nothing to do with spiritual practice may feel pressured to work for low pay because they think it demonstrates that they're more serious about spiritual practice than about worldly matters.

Associating spirituality with celibacy, isolation, and loneliness is another fear-based connection with historical roots. Monastic life is traditionally celibate, and many orders maintain silence all or part of the time. Even for non-monastics, choosing to follow a spiritual path can put you at odds with close friends and associates, who feel uncomfortable around anyone they think is "too religious." A friend told me about a man who had practiced at her Zen center for years. The senior vice-president of a major pharmaceutical company, he spent his vacations attending Zen retreats. But even after 25 years at his company, he had told no one but his secretary where he went on his time off.

Today, however, we are beginning to see hints of a future archetype that embodies the person who is simultaneously spiritual, sensual, and financially savvy. Most Spiritual Seekers and Mystics are no longer drawn to the monastic life, but we have yet to break free entirely from archetypal associations with the myths of poverty and celibacy. The contemporary Spiritual Seeker, however, is moving in the right direction. Those of you with this archetype are meant to live *in* the world, not apart from it in spiritual isolation.

Lifestyle Challenge

The spiritual path, as it is clear by now, is an inward journey. Every book on self-development you read, every seminar you attend, and every meditation you practice awakens your inner resources. Your intuition in particular becomes highly active. Intuition, or intuitive intelligence, is a subtle faculty that picks up data from the energy fields around you, converting it into the thoughts, sensations, emotions, images, and "gut feelings" that convey worlds of information to us.

There's a lot of misunderstanding about intuition in spiritual circles. But to be clear, intuition is not forecasting or mind reading—it's not a skill that predicts the future, tells you what other people are thinking, or protects you from bad investments. It's simply a built-in guidance system that is meant to keep you in inner balance. Intuition monitors your behavior, your health, and your emotional responses, alerting you to how you can bring yourself back into balance if something pulls you off. Unlike the scrambled thoughts that often run through your head, intuition is a subtle inner voice—even just a feeling—that conveys truth: "Don't eat that, it's not good for you." "Apologize for that remark, you hurt that person's feelings." "Get up and exercise, it's good for your health." "Why did you say that? It's not so."

Because the intuitive voice is the voice of truth, it can also be the source of the Spiritual archetype's anguish and stress, if you don't want to hear or feel or sense the truth that your intuition is communicating to you. We can find countless ways to turn off intuition: overeating, drugs, alcohol, loud music, busywork, clutter, sleep, and depression, to name just a few. But nothing can silence intuition forever because nothing can silence truth.

The challenge for the Spiritual Seeker archetype, then, is to awaken your intuitive intelligence. The moment you decide to fully embrace the truth and act on it, you'll feel lighter and freer, as if you've been released from a dungeon of your own making. Just as the universal lesson of the Spiritual Seeker is that the truth will make you free, the way *to* the truth is through your intuition.

Recognize Your Archetype: Are You a Spiritual Seeker or Mystic?

In fact, just about every single one of us has the Spiritual Seeker and Mystic archetypes in us. It's nearly impossible to be alive and not wonder about your life's purpose or whether there's a higher cosmic power influencing your life. (Even atheists are preoccupied with denying that such a power exists.) However, if questions of meaning dominate your life, you can safely conclude that one of the members of the Spiritual family is your primary archetype.

But which are you—Spiritual Seeker or Mystic or a hybrid of the two? If you are a Spiritual Seeker, you have the potential to walk the path of the Mystic. But do you have a yearning to give birth to a deeper life? The great majority of us aren't close to reaching the consciousness of the true Mystic, but Mystics do exist in our midst, and we may recognize them when they grace our lives. Or maybe you feel that you've blended the two archetypes and walk the path of the Spiritual Seeker/Mystic.

Check out the behavior patterns and characteristics of both the Spiritual Seeker and the Mystic to see if you recognize yourself in them.

BEHAVIOR PATTERNS AND CHARACTERISTICS OF
THE SPIRITUAL SEEKER

- You feel unsatisfied and are seeking more from your life.

- You long for happiness and health.

- You are looking for a new life direction.

- You are searching for insight into who you really are.

- You are intent on finding the meaning and purpose of your life.

- You are curious about other dimensions beyond the material plane.

- You frequently read about spiritual or philosophical ideas.

- You attend workshops and seminars on consciousness or spiritual topics.

- You have begun some form of spiritual practice, or you are considering it.

THE MYSTIC

- You are unafraid to hear, speak, and act on the truth at all times.

- You are studying with a spiritual teacher.

- You value the quality of your inner life above all else.

- You give priority to spiritual understanding over security and material concerns.

- You trust your intuition.

- You are able to step away from the material world.

- You feel humble in the face of spiritual forces.

- You are committed to a path of spiritual evolution.

- You regularly practice some form of prayer, meditation, or yoga.

Step into Your Archetype: Tapping into the Power of the Spiritual Seeker

Some of us walk the path of the Mystic. Some merely aspire to. But cultivating your inner Mystic is a lifetime process, not a concrete goal. Inner transformation requires a long-term commitment. All Mystics know that there is no end game, no arrival place.

If you're a Spiritual Seeker, new to the spiritual life, here are some suggestions for getting your toes wet:

- **Begin where you are.** It's axiomatic that the spiritual path begins right here, right now, wherever you are. You can begin your inward journey by answering some basic questions: Do you consider yourself a Spiritual Seeker? What are you seeking from your spiritual path? Is spiritual life a priority for you or more of a hobby? Take your time answering. Take all day. Take a week. What's important is to answer honestly. Look deep and really explore the thoughts and feelings that arise as you reflect on each question.

- **Be willing to change.** Nobody likes change, but we do it all the time. Consider how the spiritual journey is changing you. Who are you today? How are you different from who you were last year? Five years ago? A decade ago? Think about the choices you're making. Are they serving who you are today? Are there people, places, jobs, activities that you need to change your relationship with—or drop altogether? How can you support yourself emotionally and materially in your evolution?

- **Tell the truth.** "Of course I'm truthful," you probably tell yourself. We all do. But spiritual truth is different from not lying to your mother about where you were last night. Still, the way to deeper truth is through your everyday life choices. Speaking truth to others is being truthful to yourself.

You were born knowing truth. Connecting with it starts with listening to your inner voice.

• **Be humble.** The grace of humility can be cultivated. Start by observing how you let fear of humiliation control you. Catch yourself when you're in its clutches, scanning the room to see who might be thinking mean thoughts about you, who might send a gossipy tweet if the joke you tell falls flat. So what if no one laughs? By tomorrow, who'll remember it but you? Don't feed your paranoia. Tell yourself this truth: *No one is watching me but me.*

• **Invoke divine help.** If you've never tried prayer, give it a shot. Not just as an SOS, but as a dialogue with your divinely inspired higher self. This isn't the time to petition for a boyfriend or a Mercedes SUV. What you are really doing is opening a channel to intuitive guidance. Once you get the hang of prayer you'll find it infinitely more rewarding than making a distress call.

When you're ready to move out of a place of seeking and into the mystical life, here are some points to consider:

• **Ask big questions.** There are no small questions on the mystical path. And no one-word answers. Take time to carefully consider the following: Do you truly want to spiritually evolve? Do you have a burning need to discover your purpose above all else? Are you willing to leave your current life behind for something deeper? Are you ready to become a more conscious person, aware of both the darkness and the light within you? Are you able to make a wholehearted commitment to your spiritual evolution? Contemplate these questions as an ongoing spiritual practice, exploring what opens up for you.

• **Humility 2.0.** Humility is a grace we can never have enough of. It makes us feel a part of the human community. Humility counteracts the toxin of pride. If you're nursing prolonged anger or heartache, walk through those memories with tenderness toward all involved, yourself included. Allow yourself to view even your own pain impersonally.

- **Feeding a Mystic.** Mystics don't subsist on ferns and air. Spiritual practice is your sustenance. If you don't have a form of contemplation, find one you resonate with and practice it regularly. If sitting still is not your thing, do what Rumi did: move. He was a Sufi dervish who twirled and chanted. Or you could dance or do yoga or tai chi. The idea is to develop one-pointed concentration. When you narrow your focus, the whole universe opens up.

- **Put down your mat.** Mystics also need a quiet place for reflection. Set aside a corner for study, meditation, or yoga. Furnish it with a cushion or chair or mat. A candle and flowers are also nice. Don't make this a New Age monument that gathers dust when the novelty wears off. Invest it with your energy by using it often.

- **Be in the world.** The modern Mystic doesn't retire to a mountaintop. So how will you be with both feet in the world? This is the bliss of the Mystic: being fully present, fully open to whatever is going on—work, play, sex, traffic, noise, quiet, sorrow, joy.

Spiritual commitment is empowering. With self-discovery comes the ability to realize your full potential. Find out how you gain power and how you can regain it if you lose it.

Where You Gain Power

- **Making self-reflection a priority.**

- **Listening to your inner voice** as a guide in all matters.

- **Speaking truth** as you alone discern it.

- **Seeing failure as an opportunity** to grow spiritually.

- **Confronting inner obstacles** like fear, anger, and the desire for comfort over spiritual truth.

- **Studying the mystical laws of the universe.**

- **Remembering that every choice, every act has consequences.**

Where You Lose Power (and how to regain it)

- **Believing that being spiritual keeps you safe.** Remind yourself that like everyone else, you're subject to the ups and downs of life.

- **Betraying yourself.** Keep your beliefs and values foremost in your mind.

- **Living with chaos and distractions.** Clear your head and tidy your work and living spaces.

- **Being hooked on self-help books.** Give them to a friend and start listening to your own inner guidance.

- **Mistaking the spiritual path for the route to material success.** Right road, wrong trip. The spiritual journey is inward.

- **Fearing loneliness if you lead a spiritual life.** Start the journey and spiritual friends on the same road will appear.

Checklist for the
Spiritual Seeker and Mystic

☐ I consider spiritual awareness my highest priority.

☐ I can live my spiritual truth while walking in the world.

☐ I pay close attention to the choices I make.

☐ I rely on the guidance of my intuition, not on whichever
self-help author I happen to be reading.

☐ I will not mistake the spiritual path for the road to riches
or fame.

Final Thoughts

Our world is in need of Spiritual Seekers and Mystics. If ever there
was a time to pursue a path of spiritual truth, it's now. Have the courage to gain self-knowledge and realize your destiny. Each awakened
person can inspire many others.

CHAPTER 12

The Visionary

Archetype Family: *Visionary*

Other Expressions: *Entrepreneur, Innovator, Pioneer*

Life Journey: *To bring the future into the present*

Unique Challenge: *To remain committed to a new vision long enough to see it come to fruition*

Universal Lesson: *To believe in your vision, however great or small, and to use your creative potential to change lives*

Defining Grace: *Courage*

Inner Shadow: *Misusing your visionary power to imagine the worst possible outcomes*

Male Counterpart: *Visionary*

Myths of the Visionary: *The vision quest; futurism; the Oracle of Delphi*

Behavior Patterns and Characteristics: *The Visionary . . .*

- *breaks free of traditional expectations and rules.*
- *acts as an agent of change.*
- *relies on guidance from dreams.*
- *looks to the future and sees what could be.*

Lifestyle Challenge: *To envision new possibilities for humanity and bring the future into the present*

Life Journey

The Visionary is drawn to engaging with the future, to imagining what is possible and what might be next on the horizon. Visionaries are called so because they have a special ability to sense two forces that are constantly operating in our lives, both individually and collectively: possibilities and probabilities. Visionaries sense the changing impulses in every area of society—business and finance, social justice, medicine, science, design, fashion. Those of you with this archetype give birth to new ideas that shape the destiny of humanity. America was founded by political Visionaries who took their belief in the inalienable rights of the human spirit—life, liberty, and the pursuit of happiness—and created a template for democratic government unlike anything that had existed before. (Visionaries and Noble Rebels often go hand in hand.) These rights, they believed, were "endowed by the Creator," as the Declaration of Independence states, and therefore cannot be denied nor taken away.

Visionaries are considered the engines of change, and if you have this archetype, you provide some of the most essential ingredients required to forge a better world: inspiration, motivation, and perhaps most important of all, hope for the future. The Visionary archetype feels limited by traditional systems, constrained by conventional rules and regulations, and smothered by familiar ways of doing things.

Visionaries come in all shapes and sizes, from agents of global change like environmentalist Rachel Carson, who warned of the coming environmental crises in her masterpiece *Silent Spring*, to Visionary architect Buckminster Fuller, who decades ago saw the need for energy-efficient housing, which inspired the design of his famous geodesic dome and created a pathway for environmental architecture. Cambridge University biologist Rupert Sheldrake introduced the field of morphic resonance into the mainstream, as a result of his Visionary understanding that living creatures generate fields of conscious energy around them. Sheldrake's theories lent support to the notion of a collective unconscious shared by all humankind that was central to the work of Visionary psychiatrist Carl Jung, who introduced the world to archetypes as the psychological patterns that are the architects of our lives.

Gloria Steinem, a feminist icon, and Helen Gurley Brown, former editor of *Cosmopolitan* magazine, without a doubt are Visionaries who inspired other women to step into their power. Whether that power was radical, physical, sexual, or corporate was irrelevant. Their message was: we have choices. They envisioned a society in which women could determine their lifestyles based on their creative energies rather than simply on their biology.

New media Visionaries like Microsoft's Bill Gates and Facebook's Mark Zuckerberg turned the world upside down with their contributions to technology and social networking. Oprah Winfrey built a media empire around her vision to transform people's lives. Her school for girls in South Africa is just one example of her Visionary spirit in action.

Martin Luther King, Jr., had a vision of America without segregation, and 45 years later, we elected an African-American president. The actor Paul Newman was both a Visionary and an Entrepreneur: he gave us a new model for social enterprise when he started a company to manufacture and sell his homegrown salad dressing, Newman's Own, and other natural food products, then gave away 100 percent of the profits to charitable organizations, including a camp for gravely ill kids.

None of these people had any idea their visions would evolve into world-changing success stories. Innovations don't come with a guarantee of success. Visions and their twin, great ideas, are power seeds that are gifts from the Universe. It's up to the Visionary to plant the seed, nurture the plant, and hope that it produces an abundant yield.

Although we commonly associate the Visionary archetype with larger-than-life figures like those previously mentioned, by far the majority of people with this archetype are ordinary folk. Our vision of what could be or how we might change our world may never grow into a billion-dollar enterprise or foment a revolution, but ideas about new possibilities, however modest, are nonetheless powerful and wondrous because they represent creative ways of reimagining everyday life.

I know from years of teaching in this field that people tend to take for granted the patterns of power that shape their personalities, all of which are rooted in their archetypes. Visionaries in particular dismiss some of their most defining abilities with thoughts like *That's no big deal. I get ideas like that all the time.* For Visionaries, ideas can come so thick and fast, and they're so quick to see the hidden potential in life, that they don't even realize that everyone doesn't think the way they do. The Visionary can lose interest in an intriguing idea because she immediately gets distracted by another idea, never giving a great idea the attention it requires in order to reveal its full potential.

Perhaps you recognize yourself in that description. Or maybe you've never thought about what really drives you to be the person you are. As a Visionary you are a free-spirited dreamer, unconventional, spontaneous, and attracted to a life philosophy of endless possibilities. Your imagination is constantly picturing how things might be, or what you could do if and when the right moment presented itself.

When you're not busy dreaming up great schemes, the Visionary in you expresses itself through your highly sensitive nature. Sometimes you're so attuned to your environment that being among crowds feels as if you've just been dropped into a pressure cooker. Nonetheless, you trust your intuition although you may not always follow its guidance. By that I mean that while you lean heavily on your intuitive instincts as an organic compass, you still need to consciously choose to act upon the hunches and guidance you receive. This is true for every archetype, since intuition is a capacity we all share, but the Visionary is especially dependent upon intuition since that is the faculty she most relies on as the source of her creative ideas.

Living an intuitively integrated life can sometimes be a challenge, given the realities we face, but the Visionary continually strives to achieve a balance between rational thinking and intuition. If this is your dominant archetype, what's important for you to remember is that the intuitive self requires nurturing, and time alone on a regular basis. You need more time for reflection than you may realize, in order to keep the channel clear between your intuition and your conscious mind. That is the highway on which visions and great ideas travel, so learning to be still and listen is essential for you.

Though there is by no means a "typical" Visionary—those of you who have this archetype are as outwardly varied as any subway car full of people—what Visionaries have in common are a few very specific characteristics that position you early in life for an inner engagement with the future and a soul assignment to be an agent of change. Because the Life Journey of the Visionary is one of envisioning new possibilities, Visionaries are often outsiders as children. In all likelihood, you went through your youth feeling like you didn't fit in. Perhaps you saw the world like no one else did, no matter how small your world was back then. As difficult, even lonely, as that might have been, it shaped you into the Visionary you were to become. Not fitting in becomes your best asset as an adult. Visionaries have a unique perspective, and fitting in quite frankly would cramp your style. (Not that it's likely to happen. Find me someone who claims to be a Visionary but says she was homecoming queen of her high school, and I'll suggest she look for another archetype that more precisely describes her. The Queen might be a place to start.)

As an adult, the Visionary is driven by imagination and ideas. You are always reimagining your environment, whether your home or your business or your whole *life*, in terms of its potential. Be honest: How many times have you envisioned a new you in some way—seen yourself living a different life, in a different place? Or reconsidered your immediate environment and what it would look like and feel like if you decorated it according to the scheme you've designed in your head? Or perhaps you have envisioned a unique business idea. The Visionary sees so many possibilities in life and can't wait to give them form. People who don't have this archetype may think you're indecisive or flighty because you're constantly repainting the walls and pushing the furniture around, then updating your wardrobe and dyeing your hair to go with the stunning new interior you've created. Or they may think you are professionally irresponsible because you just can't find the right job. Visionaries, as a rule, are seeking to create their occupation, not step into an existing one.

Visionaries can't leave anything as is. They have an irresistible urge to unleash the hidden potential in anyone and everything they encounter. *Mmmm, what else could I do with this old couch or table?* a Visionary wonders, and within seconds she sees the couch reupholstered in a futuristic geometric pattern and the table repainted a vivid red. I remember hearing about a woman who dropped off a beaten-up old table and set of four chairs at a friend's house, thinking the friend might find a use for them. The table had a round glass top on an hourglass-shaped, wrought-iron base that looked like a bunch of flower stems pinched together to form a bouquet. The friend, a gifted Visionary, immediately saw potential in the table. She struck a bargain with a young art student, telling the girl that if she could find a creative way of painting the table, the Visionary would sponsor her for a class at the Art Institute of Chicago. The young artist took up the challenge, and knowing the Visionary was an avid gardener, went through her garden noting all the colors of the flowers. She then painted each chair in the shade of a flower and then painted the table base in various shades of green, as if it really were a bunch of stems with the tabletop as the floral crown.

By the time she was done, not only had this young woman produced a stunning piece of art for the Visionary, but another woman, who writes enchanting children's books about fairies, happened to see the table when she came to visit and said, "That's no ordinary piece of art. That's a fairy table, set in a perfect fairy garden. I can just see it now. It's a perfect image for a section of my book that I've been trying to write." One woman's vision inspired another person and yet another. Such is the power of the Visionary's imagination.

A Visionary of an entirely different sort is a woman I know who is brilliant at selling real estate, because she can spot the potential of a property like no one else. She didn't start out in real estate, but when an opportunity came her way to learn about urban planning, she decided to try it. She needed to finance her graduate degree in the new field, however, so she decided to make pasta and sell it on the side. In her mind, she saw herself as a great Italian cook, and it seemed logical that she could use this talent to finance grad school.

And it did. Many people see themselves in their imagination, but Visionaries take it a step further. They have what it takes to envision themselves as something out of the ordinary.

The world today is a Visionaries' paradise in that we're living at the threshold of a new era of technology and, therefore, of imagination. The Internet has awakened the Visionary spirit in countless individuals, from Larry Page and Sergey Brin, who founded Google, to Arianna Huffington, who harnessed the power of blogging in her online publication *The Huffington Post*. The Internet world is one big hothouse for Visionaries by the thousands.

The difference between Visionaries we hear about and those we don't is the willingness to set one creative idea in motion and then follow through. Sara Blakely, who created SPANX, the wonder shapewear that makes any woman—and now also any man—look, or at least feel, red-carpet ready, is a poster child for the Visionary archetype. Blakely was selling photocopiers door-to-door and moonlighting as a comedienne when she had an idea for a product she really believed in. Investors she approached didn't share her enthusiasm, but she persisted, and eventually her determination paid off. In less than a decade, Blakely had built a billion-dollar business, becoming the youngest self-made billionaire on the *Forbes* magazine list. But her vision didn't stop there. She now encourages other women entrepreneurs to follow their visions, helping support their efforts through her foundation.

Not all visions are about creating a product or something external. Some of your best ideas might be about exploring your potential as a human being. These are some of the best, most exciting visions of all. As a Visionary, you might imagine yourself on rare and unusual adventures, like going walkabout in the Australian bush or hiking the Appalachian Trail or hang gliding over Acapulco Bay. Or you might find yourself drawn to learning about holistic healing arts. Making a contribution to improving the lives of others, whether one or many, is a core value of the Visionary archetype. Visionaries are working around the globe, many of them anonymously, to make this planet a better place to live. We will never know the majority of those with the Visionary archetype who, like you, are engines of transformation in this world.

As a Visionary, your nighttime dreams are important to you: they entice you to explore the unknown—the ultimate seduction for the Visionary. Dreams are a fertile source of ideas, so you explore techniques like lucid dreaming that help you remember and even shape your dreams.

Most of your visions and ideas probably won't turn the world upside down, but they do have the potential to turn *your* world upside down. So if you feel the Visionary running through your veins, make friends with your archetype right away.

Unique Challenge

The Visionary's unique challenge is twofold, stemming from your enthusiasm for the ideas that continually pour out of your mind—and your tendency to drop a good idea before it has come to fruition. As a Visionary you are inherently in love with ideas. You love to dance with ideas, share ideas, and find ways to expand them into high-flying visions to see if they can take the altitude. An evening spent around a dinner table sharing new ideas about anything—what you're going to do next with your life, how you want to change your wardrobe, how you want to create or transform a business, how you envision a new financial future, how you want to navigate through a life crisis—has the power to lift you into a heightened state in which you feel vibrantly alive. You thrive on conversations like this, so part one of the challenge for Visionaries is to be aware of your tendency to get so caught up in the thrill of spinning out a vision that you end up talking about it rather than putting it into action.

This is the point at which part two of your unique challenge kicks in. As soon as the thrill of the moment is gone, you can come up with all sorts of reasons for not acting on your ideas. The Visionary can always find ways to poke holes in an idea, as an excuse to go in search of the *next* big idea. Perfectionists by nature, Visionaries can analyze a vision to death, deciding it would never be something as game-changing as Facebook or penicillin or the iPad, so what's the point in pursuing it?

Commitment to an idea that has the power to transform you personally in any way is a vision worth nurturing. The bottom line is, you need to remain committed to a vision long enough to see it come to fruition.

Universal Lesson

The lesson for the Visionary is to experience the power of your creative vision, however large or small, and to realize its potential in the larger scope of your life. Visionaries receive acclaim not only for what you contribute to society but also because you took a risk on something that could potentially impact the lives of many people. And you took that risk without any guarantee of the outcome. In failure, Visionaries stand alone to face humiliation and defeat. But when successful, countless people run to hang on to your podium, hoping that even the tiniest fragments of the accolades showered on you will fall their way. It's easy, of course, to praise a Visionary once her ideas have caught fire, but by that time, the *essence* of what makes a true Visionary has already done its best work. The universal lesson of the Visionary is to believe in the vision or idea itself, and in its spiritual source and its creative potential to change your life or the lives of others. Visionaries become great not just because of what they accomplished but because they had the courage to believe in the unbelievable and the impossible, even when others told them their visions would fail.

On a more personal scale, Visionaries remind us that all ideas have the power to shift the ground beneath our feet. So often people tell me that they have no idea what to do with their life or their business or their marriage. What most people are really saying, however, is that they're terrified to even *think* all the ideas rushing around in their mind because should one of those ideas take hold, their life would change forever. Change, whether personal or professional, can be extremely intimidating. Ultimately, we admire Visionaries because they are not afraid to dream big dreams and follow them, and they thrive on change.

Defining Grace: Courage

As the change agents of the world, Visionaries are continually coming up with ideas that sweep away the old and bring in the new. Small wonder then that courage, or fortitude, is the defining grace of the Visionary archetype. It takes a formidable amount of courage to be a change agent, whether you are revolutionizing an entire industry or simply opening up a new path in your personal life.

Envisioning what is possible in life, no matter the scale, means that you are recognizing that the old way is no longer working. It takes courage to introduce a new idea, as there will almost certainly be some form of opposition to it—that's the nature of change. But even a Visionary may find the prospect of change challenging when the new possibilities she's envisioning are for her own life—for who she could be and for what she might be able to accomplish if she followed through on exploring the unknown.

Understanding something of the nature of courage can help Visionaries tap into the power of this grace. If you have the Visionary archetype, it's important to remember this maxim: *Courage rises in you just as you need it most.* Courage isn't something you can warehouse when you're feeling good, then draw on later at the first twinge of fear. The grace of courage floods into you at the moment you need it. Your job is to trust that it will be there for you.

The grace of courage can help the Visionary in making the right choices. We all want to know for certain that we're making good decisions in life, but how exactly can we determine if a choice is the right one? Visionaries receive a lot of guidance intuitively. The best way to decide if you're making the right choice is to trust your gut. Really pay attention to your body and how you feel as you're mulling over a choice. Courage is the grace that continually directs you to do the right thing according to your conscience. There is no mistaking the right thing. Life is really not that complicated, but we make it so when we fight what we intuitively know because it is not convenient for us. Said differently, the wrong thing requires you to compromise your integrity. Don't you always know when you're doing that?

Inner Shadow

The inner shadow of the Visionary is misusing your visionary power to imagine the worst possible outcomes. To give you an idea of what I mean, I'll share some examples on a mega-scale. Many of you have heard of Nostradamus, a Visionary physician who, while treating people for the plague during the 16th century, wrote down numerous cryptic prophecies in the form of poetic quatrains, in order to obscure their meaning. As a consequence, his prophecies of forthcoming doom and gloom—plagues, floods, wars, and other disasters—have been interpreted and reinterpreted throughout the centuries, resulting in all manner of wildly speculative conclusions with not a shred of substantiating evidence. Modern-day interpreters have read into Nostradamus's prophecies everything from JFK's assassination to the Challenger shuttle disaster to the 9/11 terrorist attacks. If any individual stands as the quintessential shadow Visionary, it is Nostradamus, whose apocalyptic visions point to global destruction rather than human transformation.

Armageddon is a very popular theme in film, television, and video games these days, and all of these images of future worlds in which humanity self-destructs come directly from the shadow side of the Visionary archetype. The Visionary has a finger on the pulse of future possibilities, but possibilities are a coin toss, with a 50-50 chance of coming true or not. Turning the possibilities for what our world will be like tomorrow into probabilities depends upon our actions today, combined with whether or not we are optimistic and hopeful about our future. In other words, how we envision our tomorrow lays the foundation for it.

In times of great change, such as we're living in now, it's not unusual for people to feel anxiety about the future. Filmmakers, videographers, and game designers are exploiting the underlying dread rippling through the collective unconscious. The popularity of vampires, zombies, and other soulless characters from the underworld indicates how much young people today are attracted to the dark side of immortality. Filmmakers are finding ways to envision the macabre within a romantic theme—the first time we've seen this on such a grand scale.

However, Dark Visionaries have always been seductive characters in literature, film, and life. Mary Shelley's Dr. Frankenstein is a classic example. But Dark Visionaries are everywhere. I often caution people about going to psychics for personal readings because it's easy to fall under the spell of someone who senses your fears and then seduces you into thinking he has psychic insight to guide you through your difficulties. Next thing you know, you're turning to that person for every decision you make. Meanwhile, the psychic is feeding you bogus information while draining your bank account.

But the Dark Visionary doesn't just live "out there" in the world. There's a Dark Visionary in all of us that can be activated. When we envision the worst possible outcome of whatever is pending—the medical test will find a malignancy, we'll be fired from a job, our marital problems will end in an ugly divorce—that's the Dark Visionary at work. It's the shadow side of the archetype that torments the Visionary with thoughts of failure before she even tries expressing a new idea that she's been longing to give form. The intuitive Visionary, with her vivid imagination, is prone to falling into a cycle of shadow visions, until she can't tell whether what she's sensing is guidance or a product of her fear. It can be difficult to step out of this cycle, because in a paradoxical way, it's also safe: it keeps you from taking action you're afraid to take.

For the Visionary, countering your shadow side calls for cultivating awareness and observing your thoughts, so you can learn to discriminate between genuine visions and fear-based images. Fears are bullies that will hold you captive until you stand up to them. You cannot break up a fear by thinking or talking your way through it. Action is required. Courageous choices dissolve your fears, and one courageous choice inevitably leads to another.

Male Counterpart

Although archetypes are mostly inherently genderless, archetypal patterns of behavior can be shaped by the gender of the individual. In the Visionary, some of the differences can be striking.

Like the female Visionary, the male Visionary is highly sensitive and intuitive and open to new ideas. But in today's marketplace, this may make him very ambitious and competitive about getting his ideas out in the world before the other guy does. Adventure is a turn-on for all Visionaries, and most will try anything once. But while a female Visionary may get an adrenaline rush just from playing around with new ideas, a male Visionary—particularly one with a secondary Athlete archetype—may gravitate toward sky diving, bungee jumping, stunt flying, or any other sport that will literally turn him upside down and keep his head spinning.

Visionaries are comfortable with their own company—who wouldn't be, with all those exciting ideas flying around in their minds?—but at the same time, they love the sensual part of life. A Visionary man, however, may find commitment confining: boundaries and new ideas seem like opposing forces to him. And if tending to the needs of another person challenges the time and energy he needs to birth a new idea, the idea is going to win out most of the time. Male Visionaries tend to float in and out of relationships or have a relationship on their own terms. Practicality is not a Visionary strength or priority. But if a man's Visionary archetype is balanced by a more domestic one, such as the Father, he will have the blend embodied by the late Steve Jobs. Although Jobs never married his life partner, he had children with her, and their relationship was long-term.

Because they are not bound by convention, Visionary men are very innovative and forward thinking. Years ago, I met a man who ran a small manufacturing company in New England. When he noticed that his employees seemed to be feeling more stressed, he approached several staff members for feedback. It turned out that there were some newly divorced single moms who were having difficulty arranging childcare. The man had an idea, and he began looking into the possibility of providing on-site daycare, a totally novel, even risky, idea at the time. He decided to try it, however, thinking that if it didn't work out, at least he would have done his best to respond to the needs of his staff. Needless to say, the daycare program was a great success. In fact, it drew more attention of the best kind to his company than any advertising campaign ever had. This Visionary business owner demonstrated what a company could do if the leadership had the courage to take a risk. He became an inspiration to other business owners, not only because of his support for the women in his workplace but also because the daycare facility clearly demonstrated what can happen when someone sees a need, envisions new possibilities, and implements the vision.

Most visionary ideas are spontaneous, arising out of the need to resolve a situation or find a creative solution to a problem. My friend Roger is a remarkable Visionary, if not a rather accomplished eccentric, who lives at Findhorn, an ecological community in northern Scotland that has been committed to alternative living for over 50 years. A long-standing goal of the community was to create energy-efficient living accommodations. Findhorn happens to be located near the famous Whisky Trail, where popular brands like Glenfiddich and Glenlivet are manufactured. Several years ago, Roger learned that several of the distillers were switching the traditional wooden barrels in which they age the whisky to modern aluminum. He knew that these barrels were large and very sturdy, so he offered to take a couple off their hands to convert into living quarters. Within a few months, Roger's vision of living in a whisky-barrel house became a reality—a rather fragrant one, admittedly, but he had manifested his outrageous vision. Soon, other people were duplicating his barrel house, and within a few years, the area where Roger lives came to be known as the barrel-house center.

Myths of the Visionary

Myths speak to the Visionary more directly than to most other archetypes. The language of symbols and images is the lingua franca of the Visionary's inner world. The Visionary would be right at home in many traditional cultures, where knowledge is imparted through myth, story, dreams, and waking visions.

The vision quest—with its promise of transformation when undertaken with a skilled shaman, or special guide, rightly belongs in the category of visionary spiritual myths. In traditional societies, the vision quest is a rite of passage, an inner journey to awaken a seeker's visionary sense. In these traditions, the quest for inner truth and integrity is valued above all else. The vision quest awakens within the Visionary such a clear awareness of who she really is that betraying her true nature would be unthinkable from that point on. Our society does not have an exact equivalent to this experience, but those who have undertaken such a quest or a similar initiation come away with a new understanding of their life purpose. Often people emerge with a very different purpose from what they had been doing or had expected to do.

For the Visionary archetype, the vision quest is a rebirth. The Visionary, who may have been walking through our hyperrational conventional world with a sense of isolation or apartness, awakens to a deep realization that visioning—seeing what could be and bringing it to the world—is her true calling. The experience brings self-acceptance. Suddenly, the vivid dreams and visions, the attraction to the unknown, and the pull to birth her unique vision make perfect sense. The Visionary who steps into her archetype through a transformative experience of this sort finds herself, maybe for the first time ever, fully at home on the leading edge of society.

Futurists embody a very different expression of the Visionary myth. The authors H. G. Wells and Jules Verne established a precedent for imagining the coming worlds ahead, some of which, like the automatic doors and genetically engineered plants envisioned by Wells, have come to pass more or less. George Orwell, without a doubt one of the greatest futurists of all time, continues to influence from his grave with his dystopian vision, *1984*. Phrases like "Big Brother is Watching You," "Thought Police," and "In a time of universal deceit, telling the truth is a revolutionary act" have entered the vernacular, giving social paranoia a backbone. Visionary futurists like George Lucas, creator of *Star Wars*, and James Cameron, director of *Avatar*, have in common the need to tell stories about possible new worlds. In their visions, good continues to battle evil—the eternal story of humanity, only with special effects. Steven Spielberg, who dabbles in futuristic themes, captivated us with his enchanting film *E.T.*, in which he countered the stereotypic vision of violent extraterrestrial encounters with a meeting of innocence between galaxies.

Myths of the feminine Visionary make their way through figures such as the Greek goddess Athena, the power behind the thrones of men, and the Oracle of Delphi, honored by her society for her ability to reach through the veil and into the realm of the gods, to bring their messages back to earth.

Lifestyle Challenge

Great ideas come at a price. Ideas—or visions—are living creatures. When Sara Blakely imagined creating SPANX, it wasn't just an idle thought like "Let's go to lunch." Her vision was an animated download that consumed her completely. She was willing to build her life around making it a reality.

Even Visionaries can talk their visions to death, however, draining the energy from them like letting the air out of a balloon. But to bring a vision to fruition, you can't just talk about it, you have to act on it. No matter how great or modest the vision is, you have to commit to doing whatever is required to make that vision take shape. Giving form to a vision is risky business. How could it not be? You are bringing something into being that did not exist before. People who need a guarantee of success before acting on their ideas can't understand the Visionary, who will empty her bank account, max out her credit cards, remortgage her home, and sell her car—who will pour all her personal resources, in other words, into an idea whose time has come.

So if you have a vision that is begging for expression, the question to ask yourself is, *Am I willing to rearrange my life around this idea?* Whatever adjustments to your lifestyle that requires, whatever changes in your finances or living situation, are you capable of taking that type of risk? Would it scare you to suddenly get a *truly great idea?* Many of us say we'd do anything for a million-dollar idea, but if it came down to it, would we really? It's not an issue that most other archetypes will ever confront. But it's a very real question for a Visionary with an idea to put out in the world.

Even if your vision isn't one requiring bank loans and a team of investors, it requires an investment of your time and emotional commitment. Are you willing to envision a better future—whether for yourself, or for a few people, or for humanity at large—and then make whatever changes in your life are necessary to see your vision through to reality? That is the Visionary's Lifestyle Challenge.

Recognize Your Archetype: Are You a Visionary?

Seeing yourself as a Visionary can be difficult if you think the label only fits those who make radical or influential changes in the world. But an inwardly focused vision is no less worthy of the name, whether it is following a dream you've had, trusting your intuition rather than simply your intellect, or taking a chance on a new idea that changes your life in a tangible way. A vision could also take the form of imagining a change in your work or home situation. A dramatic change like moving your family to a new country to immerse them in a different culture, or leaving your corporate job to launch a new business, would be very risky if you didn't have a strong vision for how to bring it about.

But there's also the free-spirited, unconventional side of the Visionary. You love offbeat ideas and nontraditional practices. You've probably sampled any number of different spiritual practices and consciousness-raising techniques, and you're fascinated by what cutting-edge brain science is discovering about human potential. As far as you're concerned, the sky's the limit. You're a firm believer that if you can dream it, you can achieve it.

Often a Visionary can be spotted by the company she keeps. Visionaries aren't really joiners, but you do enjoy the company of other Visionaries. You're most comfortable among imaginative people with inventive ideas and an original take on life. You're drawn to—and a little in awe of—well-known Visionaries, past and present. As a child, your heroes might have been historical Visionaries like Thomas Jefferson and Ben Franklin, inventors like the Wright brothers and Alexander Graham Bell, adventurous Visionaries like Charles Lindbergh and Amelia Earhart, spiritual revolutionaries like Jesus and the Buddha, or political radicals like Gandhi and Joan of Arc. If you think about all these Visionaries, what qualities do they have that you wish you had? Can you see any of those qualities within yourself?

Maybe you're a frustrated or frightened Visionary: you dream but don't act. You're frequently inspired but quickly lose interest. You force yourself to take the safe path, but you aren't happy or fulfilled; instead you feel restless and unsatisfied. Or maybe you find yourself envisioning worst-case scenarios—poverty, failure, disappointing yourself or others—if you dare to act on your dreams. It's important for a Visionary not to get caught up in negative projections. Many of the most creative and successful innovators have a long list of things they tried that didn't work out. Do you honestly think any scientist or inventor has hit on the great solution on the very first try? I can't remember how many prototypes the Visionary industrial designer James Dyson went through before he finally hit on the design for his revolutionary bagless vacuum cleaner. Visionaries see failure as a kind of badge of courage. It means you've dared to see if one of your visions would take off.

Still not sure if the Visionary is your archetype? Take a look at the list of behavior patterns and characteristics of the Visionary on the page opposite and see whether you identify with any of them. If you feel that the description of the Visionary fits you, then proceed to the next section and discover how to fully embrace your Visionary archetype.

BEHAVIOR PATTERNS AND CHARACTERISTICS OF
THE VISIONARY

- You're continually coming up with new ideas and thinking *What if . . . ?*

- You're not intimidated by risk.

- You're an agent of change.

- You sense transformation in the outer world before it happens.

- You look for ways to break free of traditional expectations and rules.

- You've always been an outsider.

- You approach life in unconventional ways.

- You've been called an *eccentric* and a *free spirit.*

- You rely on guidance from your dreams.

- You see a problem and right away, you're thinking up solutions.

- You give yourself time alone to think and dream.

- You look to the future and see what could be rather than dwelling on what happened in the past.

- You avoid crowds when possible; sensory overload blocks your intuition.

Step into Your Archetype:
Tapping into the Power of the Visionary

Being a Visionary is no small task. It's not about reading people's minds or seeing the future so you can have an edge on your own safety and well-being. It's about grasping the big picture so you can midwife positive change.

As with any archetype, the Visionary isn't something you become; it's something you are. You don't need to pass a test to qualify. Stepping into the Visionary archetype means fully engaging with your inherent strengths. It involves learning to trust your intuition and the wisdom that comes to you from your deeper self. And although there are no courses in visioning to take, there are ways you can tap into the power of your archetype and open your wisdom eye.

- **Go on a vision quest.** In indigenous societies, one way to step into your Visionary archetype is to go on a vision quest under the watchful eye of a shaman, or spiritual guide. Some adventurous Visionaries might want to follow the traditional path. Nowadays, there are knowledgeable teachers trained in Native American and other indigenous practices who can lead individuals or groups through a journey of awakening. If you don't have the time or inclination to spend a weekend or week in the desert recovering your power animal and spirit guide, you can still take an inner journey of sorts to connect with your inner eye, the source of images and ideas. For this, you'll need to spend time alone, away from ordinary distractions, in a quiet corner at home, perhaps, or out in nature. (The woods and deserted beaches are good for this.) The point is to switch off the incessant chatter of your conscious mind and let wisdom bubble up from a deeper source.

- **Be adventurous.** Nobody can tell you to jump out of an airplane or go parasailing if you're deathly afraid of heights. But you *can* find a way to tap into your Visionary's natural affinity for adventure, even if it's just the mental adventure of learning a language or taking a course that's *way, way* out of your field. Deliberately push yourself out of your comfort zone. Navigate a city without GPS. Travel alone to an unfamiliar place where you know nobody and don't speak the language. If you're a confirmed city dweller, go camping. If you're a landlubber, spend time at sea.

- **Hang upside down.** Exercise is proven to change your brain, which changes your thoughts and mood. If you really want to loosen up your thinking and change your perspective, do yoga inversions, hang upside down from a trapeze or rings, or go bungee jumping.

- **Run with a different crowd.** This should be easy for a Visionary: you're naturally drawn to stimulating conversation and enjoy people with other backgrounds than yours. Keep putting yourself in places where you can see life through different eyes. Spend time with children and listen to what they have to say. Kids are naturally divergent thinkers, which can send your Visionary brain off in new directions.

- **Take walks.** Scientists and inventors have made some of their greatest discoveries while out walking. Letting the mind and feet wander seems to trigger brainstorms. Take leisurely walks with no special destination. Also hold one-on-one meetings on the hoof, and see how many more fresh ideas you generate than when you're sitting around a stuffy office.

• **Remember your dreams.** Dreams—waking or sleeping—are a Visionary's valuable resource, a gold mine of ideas and images with transformative powers. Keep a dream journal and work on remembering your dreams. Lucid Dreaming lets you control the course and content, so you can make the most of guidance from your deeper self and the collective unconscious.

As a Visionary archetype you pick up so much information intuitively that you want to be mindful of your surroundings. Sensory overload, especially too much noise, can prevent you from hearing your own inner guidance. Be aware of how you feel. Pay attention to what empowers you and what drains your energy.

Where You Gain Power

• **Spending time alone to dream and create.**

• **Being optimistic about the future.**

• **Cultivating the courage to act on your ideas.**

• **Sharing your visions** with people you trust who can help you put them into action.

• **Practicing some form of contemplation** to clear the channel to your intuition.

• **Giving your creativity free rein.**

• **Staying open to new ideas.**

• **Hanging out with other imaginative, visionary people.**

• **Being forthright and honest.**

Where You Lose Power (and how to regain it)

- **Buying into other people's doubts.** Ignore naysayers— they're probably just jealous. Follow a good idea and see how far it can go.

- **Dwelling on the past.** The future is your natural home.

- **Ignoring your intuition.** Before making decisions, pause and check within.

- **Giving in to fear.** Focus on what's going right, not on what could go wrong.

- **Resisting change.** You're a change agent, so take a deep breath and dive in.

- **Flirting with ideas without acting on any.** Commit to an idea—any idea. If it doesn't fly, consider it practice.

- **Trying to fit in.** Don't try to conform to an existing role or job. Create one that makes the most of your ideas and talents.

Checklist for the Visionary

☐ I pay attention to the messages in my dreams and visions.

☐ I'm always open to new people, possibilities, and ideas.

☐ I don't follow trends. I focus on innovating and creating.

☐ I think of creative ways to solve problems I see.

☐ I look to the future and say *What if?* I don't dwell on the past.

Final Thoughts

You have what it takes to make a profound difference in the world and bring about positive change. Whether you are envisioning a new you or helping others envision new lives for themselves, you intuitively come up with innovative ideas and solutions. Never doubt your irrepressible nature. Follow your dreams.

Archetype Gallery

Addict: In our society, the Addict archetype touches everyone. Aside from drugs, alcohol, food, and sex, we can be addicted to anything—work, sports, television, exercise, computer games, spiritual practice, negative attitudes, or high-risk activities that induce an adrenaline rush, as well as power, authority, control, status, fame, and fortune. Admitting addiction to a pattern or substance and then breaking its hold can be very empowering. The shadow aspect of addiction is the struggle between willpower and lack of self-control. People who are very intellectual or very emotional are linked closely to this archetype because they are skilled at rationalizing addictions. Some addictions—shopping, for example—don't seem like addictions because they're so enjoyable. But anything done to excess can turn on us. Compulsive shoppers, for example, can end up in serious debt. Just ask the Fashionista who overspends because she has to have the latest styles.

Alchemist: Historically, the Alchemist represents a futile effort to turn base metal into gold. But the highest expression of this archetype is the search for spiritual transformation. People most likely to identify with the Alchemist are those pursuing a path of spiritual development associated with the mystery schools or the study of universal laws. The shadow side of the Alchemist is the misuse of power and occult knowledge. People seeking to transform their lives are susceptible to seduction and trickery on the shadow side of magic and wizardry.

Child: The Child archetype includes many subtypes, such as the Orphan, the Wounded Child, the Innocent, the Nature Child, the Invisible Child, the Playful Child, the Stepchild, the Divine Child, and the Eternal Child. We all have aspects of the Child within our psyches, as we were all children once. If your childhood was painful, one aspect of the archetype may dominate to the exclusion of the Nature Child and Playful Child, which represent youth at its purest and most innocent. A lack of these subtypes often manifests as an inability to experience pleasure or fun. If you are habitually stressed, cultivating the Playful Child or Magical Child can help you become more light-hearted and spontaneous.

Damsel: The Damsel in Distress is an ancient archetype that recurs frequently in popular literature and film. Beautiful and vulnerable, the Damsel needs to be rescued by the Knight, who will then care for her in lavish style. Failing rescue, however, she will be obliged to awaken through a process of empowerment in which she learns to take care of herself. The shadow side of the Damsel archetype is being trapped in the old patriarchal view that women are weak and helpless and must be protected. The challenge, therefore, is for the Damsel to discover her own power and provide for herself rather than expect a man to do it for her.

Destroyer: Death and rebirth form the cycle of life, and systems and structures must be destroyed or dismantled so that new life can emerge. The Destroyer compels us to release what is harming us. But this archetype also contains its opposite, the Rebuilder, representing the power to liberate and heal. For the shadow Destroyer, destruction becomes an end in itself, a corrosive and corrupting power that can be intoxicating to wield.

Gambler: The Gambler is a risk taker who plays the odds. Expressions of this archetype aren't limited to card players and racetrack and casino junkies: day traders, entrepreneurs, even compulsive Lotto-ticket buyers also fit the profile. Energetically, gambling is a calculated risk against an uncertain outcome. On the positive side, the Gambler represents the power to trust your intuition despite others' doubts. Acting on gut instinct, Gamblers respond to guidance in the moment. Many highly successful Entrepreneurs consider themselves Gamblers, as they make risky financial investments that more conservative investors would never consider. On the shadow side, the archetype manifests as a lack of impulse control and the compulsion to continue taking risks even in the face of heavy losses.

Goddess/Heroine: Goddess worship is one of the oldest spiritual traditions, tracing back more than 30,000 years. The Goddess archetype and her more contemporary counterpart, the Heroine, embody wisdom, guidance, sensuality, physical grace, and athleticism. The shadow side of the Goddess is exploiting or overplaying your feminine power, as we see in some movie stars and fashion models.

Healer: The Healer, a companion of the Caregiver, lives to serve others by repairing body, mind, and spirit. This archetype expresses itself through a variety of practices, many of which do not involve the traditional healing arts or the treatment of disease. The Healer can be found in any occupation or role in life in which the aim is to assist people in transforming their physical or emotional pain, or in becoming whole. Essential characteristics of the Healer include the ability to channel the energy necessary to promote physical or emotional change.

Hedonist: This archetype has a voracious appetite for the sensuous pleasures of life, including food, wine, and sex but also art, music, poetry, and all the more refined offerings of society. The stereotypic view of the Hedonist as extremely self-indulgent is more a carryover from our Puritan heritage than an accurate description of the archetype. On the positive side, the Hedonist represents creative energy that embraces the very best in life and counters our archetypal fear of losing control to our libidinous instincts. The shadow of the Hedonist is the relentless pursuit of pleasure without regard for other people's well-being or your own.

Judge: You don't have to be in the judicial system by profession to identify with this archetype. If you are naturally skilled at mediating and resolving problems between people, this archetype is alive in you. The Judge inspires us to lead an exemplary life based on wisdom and temperance in our dealings with others. This is the archetype associated with the Wisdom of Solomon, referring to the biblical story that illustrates the quintessential execution of justice. Faced with two women each claiming to be the mother of an infant, King Solomon ordered that the baby be cut in two and half given to each woman. One woman said, "Go ahead, cut!" The other said she would sooner give up her baby than see it destroyed; she, King Solomon discerned, was the true mother. From that point on, wisdom and justice were bound together. On the positive side, this archetype fosters highly refined discernment and clear seeing in evaluating issues. The shadow Judge is a harsh critic passing judgment without compassion or with a hidden agenda. Sometimes this archetype is associated with suffering from having been misjudged in life, an experience that awakens the need to forgive.

Lover: The Lover archetype is expressed not just in romantic involvement but also in any great passion in life. You can be a lover of the arts, nature, cooking, or Persian carpets—anything at all. What distinguishes this archetype is a sense of utter devotion—unbridled affection for someone or something that becomes the organizing principle of the Lover's life. Physical appearance plays a strong role in the self-esteem of this archetype. The shadow of the Lover is an exaggerated and obsessive passion that undermines the person's self-esteem and physical or mental well-being.

Mediator: This archetype's virtue is smoothing relations between warring groups or individuals. The Mediator's characteristics are patience and an ability to read people and situations with laser-like focus and accuracy. Unlike the Advocate, whose strength is empathizing with those she helps, a good Mediator understands the issues on both sides of a conflict and works to bring all parties together to resolve it. The shadow Mediator has an ulterior motive or a hidden agenda and works both sides for personal gain.

Mother: The Mother is another fundamental archetype, one of the members of the Caring family. She is the life-giver, the source of nurturing, nourishment, and unconditional love. This archetype is the keeper and caretaker of the family and, as the Mother Nature archetype, acts as the protector of the earth and all life. If you are deeply committed to environmental work, this archetype may define you. When you figuratively leave storms and destruction in your wake, you are enacting the Wrathful Mother. You don't have to be a biological Mother to carry this archetype. The Mother may give birth to books or ideas, or nurture others as a teacher or chef or restaurant owner. The shadow side of the archetype may be expressed through the Abusive or Abandoning Mother.

Networker: Although networking is closely identified with the media age, the archetype is in fact ancient. The Networker's ability to forge alliances and connect disparate groups goes back to the survival skills of our earliest ancestors as they formed hunting groups and shared information on the best hunting grounds. This archetype is associated with social flexibility and empathy, which allow you to find commonality with all sorts of people. Like the related archetypes of the Messenger and the Communicator, the Networker links people via information or inspiration. The shadow Networker is self-serving, using other people for personal gain without offering anything in return.

Nun: The characteristics of this archetype are spiritual devotion, dedication, persistence, social transformation, education, and wisdom. On the shadow side, a life of deep spiritual devotion can and often does lead into the dark passages of isolation and loneliness. Today, the Nun archetype is expressed in two different ways. There is the traditional Nun, a woman who enters a convent, taking vows of poverty, chastity, and obedience. And then there is a more contemporary expression of the archetype evolving in women who have a profound need for an inner spiritual life but at the same time want an active life in the world, with marriage, children, and dynamic careers. In these women, the Nun archetype expresses as a passion for spiritual intimacy and prayer that isn't fulfilled by conventional religion and doesn't require withdrawal from ordinary life. The Nun archetype in today's world provides a template for spiritual practice rather than for a sequestered lifestyle.

Prostitute: The Prostitute archetype brings us lessons in integrity, raising issues around trading body, spirit, or identity for security or financial gain. Prostitution involves selling your talents, your ideas, or other expressions of the self as a form of selling out, of compromising your integrity. We all face the challenge of this archetype at one time or another: the Prostitute is a universal archetype representing one of life's tests. The archetype activates both conscious and unconscious feelings around seduction and control, raising questions about how willing we are to sell our own power or buy control of someone else's power. In order not to be destroyed by this archetype, we need to befriend it, seeing very clearly the choices it presents to us.

Saboteur: The Saboteur archetype comprises all the fears and issues of low self-esteem that cause us to make choices that undermine our empowerment and success. Ignore the Saboteur, and you'll fall into its shadow side, self-destructive behavior. Often we sabotage opportunities because we're not yet ready to grow or change—not ready to make a transition that would require us to leave a familiar but disempowering relationship or life situation. We may project our acts of sabotage onto others, to avoid taking responsibility for our choice to remain disempowered. As with the Victim and the Prostitute, you need to face this powerful archetype and make it your ally. Learn to listen to the Saboteur and heed its warnings to avoid behavior that will undermine yourself or others.

Slave: This archetype represents a total lack of power. The Slave has no self-authority, no ability to choose. Within a modern context, you may feel like a "psychological slave" if you have surrendered your will to those with financial authority, or an individual, or a hierarchical organization, such as a corporation or the military. For African Americans, this archetype has an immediacy others may not share. But if you think about the many ways in which this archetype can be expressed, you might not be so quick to dismiss it as irrelevant to your life. We are all slaves to the system in one way or another. But it is precisely the utter powerlessness of the Slave that is the strength of this archetype—the potential for personal transformation.

Storyteller: The Storyteller or Minstrel archetype relates our wisdom and our folly. Humankind is nowhere without our stories, telling us where we are and where we've come from. The Storyteller paints our successes and failures, fact or fiction, in broad and vivid strokes, embellishing reality so that it's less humdrum. For the Storyteller, love isn't love but passion, and personal power can move mountains. If you have this archetype, storytelling is the lens through which you view the world and your means of communicating your experience. The shadow Storyteller, on the other hand, is an exaggerator or even an outright liar. Given your imagination and way with words, it's tempting to spin information to your advantage or hide what you don't want to reveal behind a compelling tale. The challenge for this archetype is to not use your gift to mislead.

Teacher: The Teacher is the communicator of knowledge, experience, skill, and wisdom. This archetype, which embodies instruction of any kind, can manifest as parental guidance, mentoring, or modeling values like generosity and kindness. The shadow Teacher is a master manipulator, using or abusing the tutorial relationship for status or recognition. Even worse is the shadow Mentor, who imparts negative information and teaches destructive, even illegal skills, like burglary or how to cheat at work.

Victim: The Victim's negative traits are obvious, but recognizing them alerts us to when we're in danger of being victimized through our own passivity or inappropriate actions. The Victim archetype is the source of a fundamental survival instinct meant to give us "street smarts," as well as the ability to recognize when we have victimized another human being or are about to. The shadow side of the archetype is playing the victim in order to get sympathy. The Victim in us is never totally conquered, as life continually presents situations in which we have the potential to victimize or be victimized.

Warrior: The Warrior archetype represents physical and emotional strength as well as the ability to protect ourselves and defend our rights. An empowered Warrior takes up "weapons of the mind," never harming his opponent unless all other options have been exhausted. However, the shadow Warrior pursues victory at all costs, setting aside any ethical considerations, or wages war for personal gain. The Warrior archetype exists in the female psyche as well as in the male. The Warrior Woman may do battle differently because of body strength, but when it comes to having the right instincts for survival and protection, male and female Warriors are the same.

Acknowledgments

Without my dear friend, Cristina Carlino, I would never have written this book, much less have met the many wonderful people who now form the extended Archetypes, Inc. community. To you, Cristina, my gratitude and love. I consider it such a blessing to have you in my life. To my editor, Patty Gift, my endless appreciation and affection for your constant infusions of support, humor, and boundless grace. And to Hay House Publishing, my sincere love and thanks for your good faith in my life's journey. And to David Smith, my business partner of so many years, my thanks and appreciation for your skillful coordination of events early on that helped make this book happen.

A rare gift in life is to meet an individual who has a combination of lovely qualities and professional talents that perfectly defuses your stress while contributing to your creative efforts. That person for me is Margot Schupf, Vice-President, Book Publishing for Archetypes, Inc. My deepest thanks to you, Margot, and my highest regard. I could not have completed this book without you.

Writing a book can be an intense experience, especially if a writer has an especially rigorous deadline, as was the case with this book. So I want to extend a heart full of love and gratitude to my circle of forever friends and devoted family members who knew how challenging these past months were at times and jumped in to lighten the load. Small things really do matter, like spontaneous outings to a restaurant, going to a film that you never planned to see, a friend showing up just to keep you company because you've been on a writing roll for three days straight and he knows you need a break from too much time alone. (He calls it a "forced break-in"—good, huh?) You have no idea how much I appreciated your recognizing I needed time away from my computer and a few good laughs. So, with all my love, I thank Tom Lavin, Ellen and John Gunter, Bronwyn Boyle, Andrew Harvey, Meryl Martin, and Mary Neville. Special love and thanks go to Andy and Pam Kruzel and to Mitch and Marilyn Kaminski.

As always, I saved the best for last—my mom and my brother, Ed. You are my earth angels.

About the Author

Caroline Myss has been in the field of energy medicine and human consciousness for 20 years. Since 1982, she has worked as a medical intuitive, providing individuals with an evaluation of the health of their energetic anatomy system. She specializes in assisting people in understanding the emotional, psychological, and physical reasons why their bodies have developed an illness. Her *New York Times* bestsellers include *Anatomy of the Spirit, Why People Don't Heal and How They Can, Sacred Contracts,* and *Entering the Castle.* Visit Caroline online at **www.myss.com** or listen to her every week on **HayHouseRadio.com**®.

ArchetypeMe.com:
Discover the Real You

ArchetypeMe.com is a multimedia lifestyle company that brings together persona and identity in a way that excites and transforms every aspect of your life. Ready to understand your drives and interests on a whole new level? To understand your own means of self-expression? We help you to understand what drives you, better express who you are, filter the world around you more efficiently, and connect with others in a whole new way.

Visit **www.ArchetypeMe.com** to take the quiz, find your archetype, and create a life that fits.

Free e-newsletters
from Hay House, the Ultimate
Resource for Inspiration

Be the first to know about Hay House's dollar deals, free downloads, special offers, affirmation cards, giveaways, contests, and more!

 Get exclusive excerpts from our latest releases and videos from *Hay House Present Moments*.

 Enjoy uplifting personal stories, how-to articles, and healing advice, along with videos and empowering quotes, within *Heal Your Life*.

 Have an inspirational story to tell and a passion for writing? Sharpen your writing skills with insider tips from *Your Writing Life*.

Sign Up Now!

Get inspired, educate yourself, get a complimentary gift, and share the wisdom!

http://www.hayhouse.com/newsletters.php

Visit www.hayhouse.com to sign up today!

 HAY HOUSE

 HAYHOUSE RADIO *radio for your soul*

HealYourLife.com ♥

We hope you enjoyed this Hay House book. If you'd like to receive our online catalog featuring additional information on Hay House books and products, or if you'd like to find out more about the Hay Foundation, please contact:

Hay House, Inc., P.O. Box 5100, Carlsbad, CA 92018-5100
(760) 431-7695 or (800) 654-5126
(760) 431-6948 (fax) or (800) 650-5115 (fax)
www.hayhouse.com® • **www.hayfoundation.org**

***

Published and distributed in Australia by: Hay House Australia Pty. Ltd., 18/36 Ralph St., Alexandria NSW 2015 • *Phone:* 612-9669-4299 • *Fax:* 612-9669-4144 www.hayhouse.com.au

Published and distributed in the United Kingdom by: Hay House UK, Ltd., 292B Kensal Rd., London W10 5BE • *Phone:* 44-20-8962-1230 • *Fax:* 44-20-8962-1239 www.hayhouse.co.uk

Published and distributed in the Republic of South Africa by: Hay House SA (Pty), Ltd., P.O. Box 990, Witkoppen 2068 • *Phone/Fax:* 27-11-467-8904 www.hayhouse.co.za

Published in India by: Hay House Publishers India, Muskaan Complex, Plot No. 3, B-2, Vasant Kunj, New Delhi 110 070 • *Phone:* 91-11-4176-1620 *Fax:* 91-11-4176-1630 • www.hayhouse.co.in

Distributed in Canada by: Raincoast, 9050 Shaughnessy St., Vancouver, B.C. V6P 6E5 • *Phone:* (604) 323-7100 • *Fax:* (604) 323-2600 • www.raincoast.com

***

Take Your Soul on a Vacation

Visit **www.HealYourLife.com®** to regroup, recharge, and reconnect with your own magnificence.
Featuring blogs, mind-body-spirit news, and life-changing wisdom from Louise Hay and friends.

Visit **www.HealYourLife.com** today!